MW00697946

COMPANIONS
OF CHAMPLAIN

Founding Families of Quebec, 1608-1635

1613 Map of Quebec by Champlain

COMPANIONS
OF CHAMPLAIN

Founding Families of Quebec, 1608-1635

With 2016 Addendum

Denise R. Larson

CLEARFIELD

Credits

Map of Quebec:
Library and Archives Canada / nlc-000878 / FC330 C3 1613

Astrolabe:
Astrolabe (c) Canadian Museum of Civilization, 989.56.1,
photo Ross Taylor, image number S94-37602

DEDICATION

The stories of the companions of Samuel de Champlain, the families who lived, worked, survived, and endured life at an isolated trading post in the strange New World — these stories add flesh to the dry bones of the history of the seventeenth-century Age of Exploration.

The new culture that the families fashioned as they wove native wisdom with European knowledge clothed their existence with a new style of day-to-day life. No longer were they just apothecaries, merchants, carpenters, masons, and homemakers in the old cities of France. They were pioneers at river's edge and in the forests of Canada.

The small successes and touching sorrows of the new people of Quebec are the highlights of the stories of the dozen and a half families who knew and loved Champlain and shared his vision of greatness for their city. To them, this work is dedicated.

"It is indeed desirable to be well descended, but the glory belongs to our ancestors."
— Plutarch

CONTENTS

Made in 1603 in France, this astrolabe was used by Samuel de Champlain for navigation and cartography. Lost in 1613 during a difficult portage near the Ottawa River, the instrument was found in 1867 by fourteen-year-old Edward Lee. The astrolabe is now in the collection of the Canadian Museum of Civilization in Gatineau, Quebec.

INTRODUCTION

A Lost Companion

The astrolabe tumbled into the cool, mossy woods. Hidden by a web of fallen trees, covered over with browned autumn leaves, dulled by rain and snow, the navigator's tool would not see the blue horizon again for 254 years. (CMC online)

An incredibly important tool to men who ventured across the dangerous North Atlantic Ocean in the sixteenth and seventeenth centuries, the loss of his astrolabe while exploring on foot in 1613 put Samuel de Champlain and all of his companions in danger. They were forced to rely on their Native American guides to take them back to the trading post at Quebec after their excursion to the Ottawa River and the unknown and rough terrain around a series of rapids, where the instrument was lost. Champlain's chance to map the area with any precision was gone. Without the astrolabe he'd have to rely on physical observations for his log, instead of recording the celestial calculations he'd hoped to gather for his maps by his innovative use of his astrolabe on dry land.

Old friends are hard to part with. At the end of the trading season, before the snows were too deep for the hunters to bring in pelts of beaver, mink, and moose and the seas were too treacherous for safe navigation, Champlain headed back to France with some of his companions and left others to man the trading post at Quebec. He had sailed the route nine times before, but none without an astrolabe in hand. Those left behind prayed fervently that Champlain would make it to LaRochelle safely and return in the spring with food and wine and goods for trade in exchange for furs. The market for men's hats made from beaver skins was building to a frenzy in Europe, and mercantile companies wanted to cash in on the craze, which lasted until a change in fashion, always a fickle master, demanded silk hats for men. (White Oak)

Resurrection

The year 1867 would be a pivotal year for fur, the former New France, and happenstance. In that year the bottom fell out of the market for animal pelts for use in men's hats and other pieces of European apparel. The fur trade between Native Americans and Europeans, between North America and Europe virtually ended. By means of the British North America Act, Upper Canada (Ontario) and Lower Canada (Quebec), New Brunswick, and Nova Scotia united in a confederation called the Dominion of Canada. By the shores of Green Lake in newly designated Ontario, inquisitive Edward Lee pulled from forest debris a circle of metal with a rotating cross arm. Curious to know what it was, he showed it to his father, who was clearing trees from the land around the lake. Champlain's astrolabe once again saw the light of day. (CMC online)

The simple astrolabe unearthed by that youth near a northern lake had slept through the founding of a French enterprise and the expansion of English settlement, the passing of Champlain and his devoted companions. It rose from leaf litter, soil sediment, and mossy coverlets to be greeted by thousands of descendants of those four dozen companions and just in time to view the confederation of a new Canada.

❄ X ❄

CHAPTER ONE

Westward to Fish and the Far East

The turn of the century between the sixteenth and seventeenth was a time of scientific discovery, exploration, and empire building, an age of invention and adventure. New developments in maritime navigation, not to mention the well-publicized adventure of Christopher Columbus at the close of the fifteenth century, inspired the powers of Europe to venture to the west to look beyond the long, dangerous land routes to the spice markets of the Far East and to follow the fish.

Providing sufficient amounts of food, especially fish, was at times a big concern in France. During the Renaissance, the Catholic Church, which had in its own way preserved western culture during a very dark, vulnerable time, after the fall of Rome ca. 400 A.D., gradually came into almost omnipotent power with good — if somewhat misguided — intentions. Gradually, the number of days decreed to be for fasting for the salvation of the soul — and damnation if anyone didn't fast — were added to and multiplied by church rulers until one hundred fifty-three days a year were days of fast. Wednesdays, Fridays, Saturdays, all of Lent and Advent were off-limits to the eating of flesh. Some considered fowl as well as fish to be acceptable substitutes to red meat, but most adhered to the fish-only policy. (Fletcher 51, 93) (Lanctot 76)

Cod of the cold, northern waters was what the majority of the people of the sixteenth and seventeenth century ate on fast days. Merchants supported fishing communities, and fleets followed the cod across the Atlantic. The fish colonies were slowly migrating towards Greenland and North America in response to changing weather conditions and water temperatures during the Little Ice Age, which peaked at the turn of the sixteenth century into the seventeenth. The French fishing fleet followed the fish to the Americas during the 1500s. Explorers, with the backing of the monarchies, in turn followed the fishing fleet west, in search for a water passage to the Far East. (Fagan 103)

There is a famous story about the maitre d'hotel Vatel who committed suicide because the fish that had been ordered for a feast for Louis XIV, given by the Prince of Conde in 1671, did not arrive on time. What most people don't realize is that the day of the grand banquet was a Friday, a day of fast. The great and powerful did not forego festivities just because the Church decreed a fast day; but they, and even the king, towed the line about not eating meat. At the feast for Louis XIV, fish, by default, had to be the dominant food, the centerpiece. Without fish, the table display would have been humiliating and the courses, sparse, something Vatel could not bear to see, and so he ended his culinary career — permanently. Sadly, the fish arrived shortly after his desperate act.

For the foods that could not be eaten fresh or dried as easily as fish, there was great demand for flavor enhancements in a very big way. With no means of refrigeration, pepper and nutmeg were the favored spices used to mask the off-taste of spoiling meat, which was too scarce and expensive to throw away.

During Columbus' time, Venice was the sole outlet in Europe for the spices of India, thanks to a trade agreement between the Venetians and Arabs that dated to the seventh century. When the Turks made war and closed the overland route in 1453, the price of pepper, a very valuable commodity, shot up thirty fold. (Dugard 23)

So valued was pepper that, centuries later, a peppercorn or two still could be used as legal tender in England and New England as symbolic payment when two organizations, such as a town and a private school, transferred property between them. Pepper was favored above other spices for its ability to mask the taste of spoiled meat. Salting, smoking, or submerging meat and fish in brine were the common methods of preserving food before the invention of refrigeration, but the process was not always successful nor tasty. Food was too expensive and hard to obtain for any of it to go to waste. Pepper, nutmeg, and herbs were used in abundance to make the preserved meat palatable. The demand for spice went far beyond a desire for seasonings.

At the time of Columbus' voyages west, a pound of nutmeg could be exchanged for seven fattened oxen. (Dugard 24)

About a decade before Champlain's first excursions, a Greek pilot by the name of Juan de Fuca claimed to have sailed the Strait of Anian from the Pacific Ocean to the North Sea in Europe. This played into the mistaken belief held by most European monarchies that there was a northwest passage across the newly discovered Americas that connected the Atlantic and Pacific oceans. The myth of such a waterway was not dispelled until the eighteenth century by the comprehensive explorations and detailed records of men such as James Cook, George Vancouver, and Alexander MacKenzie.

Monetary Incentives

Though Samuel de Champlain used the newest navigational methods to chart a course, Henry IV and the mercantile associations of France did not send men like Cartier and Champlain out to make scientific studies and discoveries. Expeditions were sent to find a sea route to India and China, to look for a way to make a quick buck, a fast fortune in exotic imported goods. Spain, Holland, Portugal, and England were staking claims on territories in the New World with the intention of controlling access to any inland water route to distant trading centers.

Champlain wrote in his journal on one of his early voyages, "One may hope to find a short route to China by way of the river St. Lawrence; and that being the case, it is certain that we shall succeed by the grace of God in finding it without difficulty; and the voyage could be made in six months; whence a notable profit may be gained such as the Portuguese and other nations derive, who go to the Indies." (Biggar 345)

The explorers were also to keep sharp watch for gold, minerals such as lead and copper, and gemstones and report on any sea serpents they encountered. The race for easy wealth was on.

New Technology

Just a scant eleven years before Champlain was commissioned to found a trading post at Quebec in New France in 1608, Galileo in Italy invented the geometric and military compass based on the magnetic compass devised in China; and a year after Quebec's founding, in 1609, Hans Lippershey in Holland devised a spyglass. Galileo would later improve on Lippershey's invention and grind lenses to X20 and use the improved glass to identify ships at sea and study the moon and stars.

Champlain, a cartographer and navigator by trade, is not known to have invented any scientific instruments, but he was a pioneer in the use of new developments in maritime technology, including the astrolabe, compass, and speed log. His own astrolabe was a new model, made in 1603, just ten years before it was lost in the Canadian woods. Versions of the astrolabe had been used since 170 B.C. to track celestial bodies in order to determine Earth latitude and time. The Arabs used astrolabes to sail coastal waters. It wasn't until the sixteenth century that Europeans devised a simpler astrolabe for use by long-distance mariners who would sail beyond sight of land.

Finding Latitude

One of the most crucial yet complex elements of calculating location by the stars is the length of a degree of latitude. By Eratosthenes' calculations, a degree would be 127.7 kilometers. By those of Columbus, it would be 83 kilometers. In 1525, thirty-three years after Columbus landed on the western coast of the Atlantic, Jean Fernel set out in his carriage, determined to find the exact length of a degree.

Fernel measured the circumference of one of the wheels of his carriage then drove very slowly north from Paris, counting every revolution of the wheel. Seventeen thousand and twenty-four revolutions later, he arrived in Amiens. Having "shot" the sun with a quadrant, a simple version of the astrolabe, to find his location north of the equator before leaving Paris, he repeated the procedure in Amiens. The two cities being nearly one degree of surface arc apart, he deduced that one degree was approximately 110.72 kilometers (about 69 miles). His calculation was within spitting distance of the exact measurement. (Wilford 94-95, 98)

Other methods of determining the location of a vessel at sea were just as simplistic as Fernel's carriage jaunt. Ship's compasses of the era were little more than a magnetic needle floating in a bowl of water in the binnacle, a protective casing. The Spanish were the first to use the instrument successfully to circumnavigate the globe in 1522 in the 85-ton Victoria. (The tonnage of a ship was not the weight of the vessel, but the number of wine casks, called tuns, that could fit in a ship's hold. A tun was about a yard across and a yard and a half long. [Dugard 116])

By Champlain's time, the compass was still far from perfect. The needles often became demagnetized and readings were made erratic at times by unknown forces. The shape of the needle underwent many transformations and ranged from a simple sewing needle to a flat diamond shape, two wires bent to form a diamond and, finally, a simple bar of iron.

To figure out how fast a ship was traveling along its course, a speed log was thrown overboard. The original speed log, a large piece of wood, was thrown overboard and timed as it passed along the side of the ship, with the speed calculated as to how fast the ship took to pass the log from stem to stern. The first known illustration of a more sophisticated ship's log used to measure its speed was sketched by Champlain and used in the 1632 edition of his work "Le voyages de la Nouvelle France Occidentale." Champlain's log was a piece of wood carved to accommodate a lead weight and suspended by three short lines that were attached to a long line that was knotted at every 48 feet, which equaled eight fathoms. Cast overboard, the log stayed on the surface of the water and the line played out for half a minute, as timed by a sandglass. At the end of the 30 seconds, the line was held and hauled back in. The number of knots that had played out in the half minute was the nautical miles per hour at which the ship was running. (Gurney 24-25)

The Mettle of a Man

Champlain was a mariner by trade and put all the latest scientific techniques to use. Yet he knew that the instruments were only as good as the man who used them. In his "Traitee de la Marine, et du Devoir d'un bon Marinier," (Treatise on Seamanship and the duty of a Good Seaman), Champlain wrote:

"He must be in readiness for ordinary dangers ... But when misfortune bringeth you to such a pass, that is where you must display manly courage, mock at death though it confront you, and in a steady voice and with cheery resolution urge all to take courage and do what can be done to escape the danger, and thus dispel fear from the most cowardly bosoms; for when they find themselves in a hazardous situation, everyone looks to the man who is thought to have experience, and if he is seen to blanch and giveth orders in a trembling and certain voice, all the rest lose courage. Often one hath seen ships lost in situations from which they might have got clear had the men seen their captain undaunted and resolute, giving orders boldly and with authority." (Morison 237, 244)

Men, Machines, and Money

Champlain and his financial backers for exploration and settlement did not have the full backing of the men most influential with Henry IV, which slowed government support and funding, things that, even at the best of times, are not fast moving. Arrangements for settlement in New France was not a governmental undertaking, money being short and the enterprise chancy. Henry IV decided to follow the example of the Dutch and established trading companies for colonial enterprises, one in 1604 to the East Indies and one in 1605 to New France. Commercial companies as authorized by Henry IV would be the major backers for what was considered a mercantile venture. France was not in the business of seizing and settling large tracts of land far removed from the motherland. (Greengrass 175)

Henry IV's strengths ran in compromise and grand design, but not financial planning, and this led to limited support for posts in Canada. His negotiations and final settlement between Catholics and Protestants in France and peace with England and Spain sapped the royal treasury and created massive government debt. Yet he thought that peace was well worth the price and that economic hardships were easier to bear than death, destruction, and despair.

Champlain was not Henry's equal in diplomacy in New France, though he could have been if given enough troops and financial backing. Champlain aligned his fledgling enterprise with the native Micmac and their related tribes against the more aggressive and unpredictable Iroquois. Had there been more support from back home in France, the Iroquois uprisings and attacks most likely could have been crushed or warded off altogether. Unlike Henry, Champlain could not create endless debt and taxes to pay it. He had to make do with the meager issue of men and supplies grudging doled out by Henry's ministers, who were not entrepreneurs or speculators of any sort.

Power Behind the Throne

Maximilien de Bethune, Baron de Rosny, Duc de Sully (1559-1641) was Henry's right hand man and a homebody. After taking office as Henry's finance minister, Sully managed to reduce France's debt almost by half in ten years. By 1608, the year Champlain got the go ahead to build a permanent trading post in the wilds of New France, things were looking up. Henry was an armchair adventurer who wanted to see development of trade with the Far East along the shortest, fastest route, which was believed to lie along the waterways of the New World. The Portuguese and Spanish had already sent out numerous expeditions to find and control such a route to the rich markets of India and China, and Henry wanted to be in on the race to riches.

Sully, however, was of a different mind. He motto was, "Le labourage et le pastourage, voila les deux mamelles de la France, les vraies mines et tresors du Perou." In other words, industry and farming at home are the real treasures, not dreams of great wealth in the Americas. If left up to him, he would leave Mexico and Peru to Spain and North America to England and they would be welcome to it. There is little doubt that Sully's attitude and influence on Henry and the country's finances directly impacted the amount of seed money begrudged to Champlain and the mercantile organizations that underwrote him and the workers who accompanied him. Sully saw little purpose in settling a faraway land separated from France by a cold, wide, wild sea. He had his own agenda that called for rebuilding and renovations throughout France. It is he that the French can thank for the charming and convenient network of canals and bridges, the lovely roadways lined with trees, and renown textile and glass industries. The latent wealth of fish, furs, and forest in far away New France did not tempt Sully. They were commodities he wisely knew he could not control without great outlays of money for development and protection against the competing Dutch, English, Portuguese, and Spanish, just to name the major players. He invested the country's resources in a sure thing in the hopes of bringing France back to its greatness without counting on dreams of discovery or an uncertain enterprise.

Dismissing New World colonies and speculative ventures, Sully relied on the amazingly fertile fields and pastures of France to improve the economy and set the country on its feet. He strengthened or rebuilt 36 fortresses along the frontiers of France, from the Mediterranean Sea to Flanders, within a space of about 20 years, ending in 1610 with the death of Henry IV. (Horne 117)(Greengrass Map 3)

Sully was willing to direct funds to build domestic industries to produce tapestries, carpets, cabinetry, glassware, ceramics, and clocks to solve France's monetary problems at the turn of the sixteenth to seventeenth centuries. The fame of Lyon silk and Gobelins tapestry in Paris spread throughout Europe. He even went so far as to encourage the nobles to be involved with trade and started the seeds of professional mercantilism through his enthusiasm for guilds and corporations, but he was loath to speculate beyond France's borders. (Greengrass 176-177)

Not helping in his opinion of the New World was the blunder by Jacques Cartier in 1534. Cartier, commissioned by the king of France to look for gold in the Americas and a water route to Asia and its markets, sailed along the great St. Lawrence River and found what he thought were gold and diamonds. His men loaded barrels of the minerals onto the ship, along with some furs gotten in trade with the native Micmac, and returned to France, declaring they had claimed a land of great wealth for the glory of France. When the supposed gold and diamonds tested out to be nothing more than iron pyrites and quartz, Cartier, and thus France, suffered humiliation. The incident gave birth to the French idiom, "false as Canadian diamonds," a phrase Sully must have heard as a boy and heeded as a man. (Trudel 48)

Of like mind was the great philosopher Voltaire, who, when the English General Wolfe prevailed on the Plains of Abraham in 1759, would dismiss the loss of Canada as only "a few acres of snow." (Horne 117)

Giving weight to Sully's argument was the discovery that North America, though on the same latitude lines of France and the Mediterranean, did not benefit from a similar climate. Maine sits on the same latitude as France, but the only remarkable similarity weather wise is the quality of sunlight, which is renown with artists in both locations. But the pines of Maine and the palms of Nice are not so similar.

England was eager to colonize lands just south of France's claims in the New World with hopes of establishing plantations of olive trees and exotic fruits to reduce imports from Italy and Spain. Instead, planters in Virginia had to turn to tobacco for their enterprise.

Samuel de Champlain saw potential in the vast forests of New France. Traveling across the North Atlantic almost annually, he continued to urge the mercantile backers to send more people and supplies to the struggling trading post. He stood as a solid cornerstone to the founding of Quebec in 1608, well deserving of his designation, Father of New France. But he was not alone.

CHAPTER TWO

The Pioneers of New France

Acadia

Sam Champlain had some practice in the art of sailing across the turbulent Atlantic Ocean. The son of Antoine Champlain, a ship captain, and Marguerite LeRoy, he sailed in 1599 to Spain and the West Indies while in his twenties and worked his way up to navigator and cartographer to Pierre du Gua de Monts, who was appointed lieutenant-general of the lands of New France.

Neither Champlain nor de Monts had much experience in wintering in New France. Their 1604-05 attempt at establishing a trading settlement on an island between what is now Maine and New Brunswick was a disaster. (Tanguay 8)

In 1604, De Monts and his subordinates approved of St. Croix Island in the river known by the same name as the site for a trading post. They would rue the day. Attacked by scurvy rather than the natives, held captive by dangerous ice floes clogging the river and blocking access to the mainland, more than half the men were dead by spring.

The survivors and reinforcements relocated to a peninsula in Acadia, present day Nova Scotia, in 1605. The traders had reliable access to the mainland and its water and food sources and were not cornered again by a harsh winter.

Using ice cores, tree rings, records of wine harvests, and historical accounts, geologists have judged that the Little Ice Age was upon Champlain, his companions, and most of the world north of the equator. The year 1601 had been the coldest since 1400 in the northern hemisphere, somewhat due to the volcanic eruption of Huanyaputina in Peru. Not a threat as obvious as an encroaching glacier, the Little Ice Age was a series of erratic, extreme, and rapid climatic changes that generated frequent and violent ocean storms, devastatingly cold winters alternating with mild, snowless ones, and saturating months of rain. (Fagan xiii, 51)

Canada

Late spring was a good time of year to sail the Atlantic. Champlain, aboard Le Don de Dieu (Gift of God), sailed from the port of HonFleur in France April 13, 1608, and arrived at Tadoussac June 3, 1608. Anchoring the large vessel at Tadoussac, Champlain and his crew continued up the river in sloops. They pulled ashore below the high hill overlooking the river on July 3, 1608. (Morison 102)

The village of Stadacona had once stood on the mount overlooking the river but had been destroyed during intertribal wars. The immediate region was called by the natural feature of the narrowing of the river, which in the native language sounded very much like "que-bec," and it continued to be so called by Champlain and his men. (Lanctot 103)

"From the island of Orleans to Quebec is one league, and I arrived there on July the third," wrote Champlain. "On arrival I looked for a place suitable for our settlement, but I could not find any more suitable or better situated than the point of Quebec, so called by the natives, which was covered with nut trees. I at once employed a part of our workmen in cutting them down to make a site for our settlement, another part in sawing planks, another in digging the cellar and making ditches, and another in going to Tadoussac (where the ships were anchored) with the pinnace to fetch our effects. The first thing we made was the storehouse, to put our supplies undercover, and it was promptly finished by the diligence of everyone and the care I took in the matter. ... I continued the construction of our quarters, which contained three main buildings of two stories. Each one was three fathoms long and three wide, with a fine cellar six feet high. All the way round our buildings I had a gallery made, outside the second story, which was a very convenient thing.

"There were also ditches fifteen feet wide and six deep, and outside these I made several salients which enclosed a part of the buildings, and there we put our cannon. In front of the building there is an open space four fathoms wide and six or seven long, which abuts upon the river's bank. Round about the buildings are very good gardens, and an open place on the north side of 100 or 120 yards long and fifty or sixty wide." (Biggar, 24-25, 35-36)

At present day, the church Notre Dame des Victoires stands on the site of l'Habitation, which is what Champlain called the main building in the settlement. (Lanctot 110)

Defense was a crucial part of survival in the early seventeenth century, both in Europe and in the wilds of Canada. While Sully was in France building or reinforcing three dozen fortresses along national borders, a few hale and hardy Frenchmen were constructing Fort St. Louis atop Mont Diamant in Quebec. The hotel Chateau Frontenac stands on the site today. (Greengrass 296)

The work on Quebec was slow but promising.

"As for the country itself, it is beautiful and agreeable, and it brings all sorts of grains and seed to maturity," Champlain wrote in his book "Voyages." "There are in it all the varieties of trees we have in our forests on this side of the ocean and many fruits, although they are wild for lack of cultivation, such as butternut trees, cherry trees, plum trees, vines, raspberries, strawberries, gooseberries and red currants, and several other small fruits, which are quite good.

"There are also several sorts of useful herbs and roots. Fish are plentiful in the rivers, along which are meadows and game in vast quantity. From the month of April until the 15th of December the air is so healthy and good that one feels in oneself no tendency to sickness; but January, February and March are dangerous for the maladies which prevail ... (scurvy from salted meat, no fresh produce)" (Biggar 60-61)

Interaction with the Native People

Champlain and his men never did seem to develop a taste for sagamite, a mash made by the native people with corn flour and oil or grease, fish or meat and berries, and said to taste like wallpaper paste. It was cooked in waterproofed birch bark containers or animal skin sacks into which stones heated in a fire were dropped — an authentic stone soup. Hollowed soapstone or wooden trenchers held the sagamite at meal time. (Lanctot 15-16)

Some tribes grew and harvested what is referred to as the three sisters — corn, beans to grow up the stocks, and squashes and pumpkins to grow around them and cool the roots. Wild rice and sunflowers were gathered. Tobacco was grown but was used only by the men and jealously guarded.

Travel for the Europeans and native people was limited to paths through the woods and by canoe on rivers and lakes. Birch-bark canoes were strong, long, and made for transporting people and goods. The canoes were framed with cedar timbers and struts and covered with birch, pine, and elm bark pieces that were sewn together with flexible roots and waterproofed with pine resin. The craft and all its contents had to be carried from one waterway to another at portage points, called carrying places.

The Europeans did not sit idle in Quebec, waiting for native hunters to bring in the furs. Voyageurs, which translates as travelers, were agents from the trading post who negotiated with the native people for furs. The voyageurs traveled by canoe to meeting places upriver to conduct the trade. They would then transport the furs to Quebec, and later to Montreal, for loading on ships to France.

Coureurs des bois, translated runner in the woods, were unauthorized traders who made deals on their own with the native hunters and sold furs to the highest bidder, sometimes French but often English or other nationality. The French government bitterly denounced as traitors these entrepreneurs who ignored the trade monopoly.

Quebec, a Remote Outpost

A few members of the Third Estate, professional people not of the nobility nor the clergy, were part of the contingent establishing the Quebec post. Among these were Louis Hebert, a former apothecary to the royal household. His skills as a physician and pharmacologist and were important to the success of the venture. His dwelling, near the fort on the promontory, was constructed of stone and was a gathering place. (Lanctot 110)

In time, men would bring their families to Quebec, but the mercantile companies funding the post wanted profit, not settlement. Champlain, in near disgust, wrote in his journals, " ... reaping riches for the greater profit of the company (Company of Merchants) ... was the sole concern of the company which ... wholly neglected the peopling of the country, and continually sought to earn as much as possible for the least possible expense." (Lanctot 119)

Hebert's contract with the Company of Merchants, also called the Company of Canada, was for two years at 300 livres a year, the median income at the time. His duties were to care for the sick and do what was required for the betterment of the people. Under the terms, he was allowed to work his land during his free time but any produce would belong to the company for the first two years. After that, any excess production beyond what was needed for his own family would have to be sold to the company, which would then sell it to the Europeans, not the native people, at the rate currently charged in France. Louis is called the first farmer of France and is often portrayed with using a plow, but he never had one. The company would not allow the importation of a plow, lest the Heberts go into business for themselves. (Trudel 124)

Respect for the law as well as the long arm of the company had come ashore with Champlain, who was in charge of the settlement, and his companions. The terms of the contract, as restrictive as they were, were abided by Hebert, his wife, Marie Rollet, their three children and his brother-in-law Claude Rollet. This conformity paid off. In 1623 Hebert was granted a concession for his land atop the promontory of Cape Diamond. In 1626, his estate was raised to the status of noble fief by the viceroy, Levy de Vantadour. Hebert was also granted a second noble fief on the St. Charles River, near the fief of the Recollects. (Trudel 134, 139)

The men persevered, the women and children came, but only a few. "There were but five families of workmen truly settled in the country (in 1628), namely the Desportes, Martin,

Pivert, Hubou and Foucher families," Champlain wrote. "Only two families, that of the widow Hebert (Louis had died after a fall from scaffolding while trying to repair the roof of his house January 25, 1627) and her son-in-law Guillaume Couillard, were working the land — tilling two lots among them, or seven acres in all" (Lanctot 122)

After twenty years, few inroads were made in the development of a city as Champlain had envisioned. For want of backing, Quebec remained a remote bartering center with a transient population of seventy-six clerks, interpreters, employees such as Louis Hebert, servants and missionaries. A humble showing for a world power like France, but it was the powers back home, both the Company of Merchants and the royal government officials, who held the purse strings and kept them pulled tight, making only minimum expenditures. (Lanctot 126)

Permanent settlement, as in a people taking over the land and becoming self sufficient and making a profit from agriculture, was extremely slow. Produce for shipment back to France was not an issue for the Company of Merchants that was funding Quebec. France, in spite of a sluggish economy, was a very fertile and productive country. Sending people across the Atlantic to farm and then shipping stuffs back was not profitable. The people who decided to stay in Quebec for better or worse cleared enough land to satisfy their own needs. Two religious groups, the Recollets and the Jesuits, established farms to feed themselves and assist the native people they tried to convert, yet they managed to clear and plant only 15 acres in 20 years. (Lanctot 122)

Sticking to Business

The mercantile companies were adamant about discouraging large-scale farming. It was not until 1628 that a plow was pulled through Canadian soil for the first time. The companies feared that settlement of the land would drive away both the fur-bearing animals and the hunters who brought in the pelts for trade, which was very, very profitable in the seventeenth century. As the economy in France recovered under the tutelage of Sully, more money was spent on luxuries, including beaver-skin hats. The velvety pelt of the North American beaver was in great demand in Europe and the markup from hunter to hat was phenomenal. At a time when 15,000 to 20,000 beaver furs were traded a season, one pelt was purchased for three livres in Quebec but sold to a dealer for 10 livres in France, who would then resell it to hatters for turning into a retail commodity. (Lanctot 124)

The mercantile companies calculated how many families would be required to sustain the fur trade and how many soldiers would be needed to protect them — about 300 — and were loath to send out more than that. The mission of the company was not to conquer or convert but to conduct commerce. The manufacture of goods of any sort was out of the question. Motherland France had a strict monopoly on that. (Morison 172-4)

Only the fabrics and knits — capes, blankets, nightcaps, hats, shirts — metal tools, such as awls, hatchets, knives, and iron arrowheads, and dried fruits and peas that were used as barter with the native hunters were shipped in great quantities to Quebec. The materials were cheap in comparison to the luxurious pelts of beaver, moose, lynx, fox, otter, marten, badger, and muskrat that were traded in exchange. The native people eventually caught on through trade with other Europeans that the furs were of greater value than they were led to believe and demanded more substantial goods in exchange, including weapons; but at the beginning, business was good for the mercantile companies, and they were loath to have it change. To the majority in France, Canada meant little more to them than a "summertime trading post" and there was little mention of it in contemporary literature and records. (Morison 188) (Lanctot 122-23)

The mercantile company that took over in 1627, Compagnie des Cent-Associes, the Company of 100 Associates, did little better than its predecessor. Each member of the company contributed 3,000 livres, which was about ten times the average annual wage in France, and had to agree to reinvest most of the profits back into the company. Though granted a monopoly for all trade except fishing for fifteen years, there were numerous setbacks and losses, and the company lost its monopoly in 1632 to the deCaen family and the right to any and all trade in Canada to the Communaute des Habitants in 1645. Trade and profit was foremost in the minds of the company members. When their profits slowed or failed to come in — which often happened — they delayed or fully neglected the agreement to transport 4,000 settlers to New France within set periods, arguing that there was no money with which to do it. Those who did voyage to the colony could only hope that the annual resupply shipments would be sent and would reach them.

Why They Went to Canada

The men who sailed to Quebec with Champlain were not sent to seize and occupy great tracts of land for themselves or France. The Company of Merchants and later the Compagnie des Cent-Associes (aka Company of New France), which assumed the supervisory role in 1627, funded the trading post and wanted minimum disruption of the natural habitat and the native hunting parties to keep the shipments of animal pelts flowing to Europe. The native hunters soon developed their own agenda for the fur trade and used their knowledge of the land and warring tribes to prevent the Europeans from establishing trading posts farther west. The natives wanted to maintain their monopoly on the supply of furs from western tribes to the Europeans on the coast.

The company was obligated to send annual shipments of goods from the ports of France to Quebec. Commonly stowed aboard were barrels of peas, beans, rice, prunes, raisins, almonds, dry cod, salted meats, flour for bread and biscuits, spices, sugar, salt, oil, and butter. For refreshment, the company sent casks of cider and beer from Normandy and wine and spirits from mid and southern France (Lescarbot 91; Trudel 152)

The settlers supplemented their stores when opportunity arose. They planted the seeds of old-world vegetables after clearing some land and traded with the native people, who grew corn and pumpkins and gathered berries and maple sap. Both natives and newcomers hunted bear, duck, geese, moose, and turtles and caught fish. The native men were adept at catching river fish and eel.

On special occasions, the small populace pooled what they had. "For the feast of the spring of 1627, everything was thrown together to cook in Mistress Hebert's great (beer) brewing cauldron," an early report of the post remarked. It's doubtful that Mme Hebert made sagamite, a native mix of cornmeal and anything on hand that was edible; or migan, a boiled mix of maize and often old fish. Champlain thought both dishes smelled and tasted terrible. For their part, the natives liked French peas and craved bread made with the flour sent from France. They had cornmeal, but that was used as a cooking ingredient and not made into cakes. (Trudel 152-3, 160)

So why did the men and their families stay in a primitive and at times menacing environment, so much colder than la belle France and far away from civilization as they knew it? Perhaps that civilization was not so civilized nor safe. Wars of greed, revenge, and religion were frequent in sixteenth and seventeenth century Europe. The burden to wage war was loaded onto the backs of the working people. There were taxes at every turn and taxes of every kind. There were the taille, the corvee, and the sabelle taxes. There was a tax, en censive, at each transfer of ownership and taxes for the tenant farmers, the censitaires. Farmland in France was extremely expensive. Land in Canada could be had for the clearing if so granted, and was tax free. So were the people — free from social strictures placed on them by a class-conscious society and a powerful clergy, free from religious rivalries, except what was brought along by the Catholic and Huguenot clergy. The clergy's mission, however, was the conversion of the native people, and ministering to the emigrants was secondary.

The outdoor life of hunting and fishing was a siren to the men of France who had been limited to cities or small farms while vast estates were held by the king and the nobility. Craftsmen who would have waited many years for masters papers in Europe were promised master standing after just a few years' labor, about six, at the Quebec post. They were willing to take their chances with the long Atlantic crossing, possible seizure by ships flying the flag of competing or warring Europeans, occasional attack or ambush by the Iroquois, the hard work of clearing land thick with hardwoods and pine, and the disinterest of the merchant companies and the French government.

Benign neglect suited these pioneers. They were on their own, beyond the reach of old-world ways and restrictions. Life was good — simple but good — with increased potential for prosperity of a self-directed nature. Until Captain Kirke arrived.

Always the Gentlemen — the Brothers Kirke

The English knew all about New France. Just a year after Champlain and his men started a serious establishment in Quebec, Richard Hackluyt took a manuscript to P. Erondelle in London for translation from French to English. The text of the 1609 translation is in early modern English, the language of Shakespeare. Hackluyt wanted to share with English sailors the sailing directions that Champlain had compiled during earlier explorations along the coast of Acadia and Canada. The text often parallels Champlain's accounts in his "Voyages." (Lescarbot)

In 1627 the brothers Kirke set sail from England for New Foundland, sent there by Charles I. Two years later, in 1629, during a rare moment of peace between England and France, the Kirkes sailed up the St. Lawrence, supposedly at the bidding of the English king. They didn't need an astrolabe to find Quebec, sitting above and below a promontory where the river narrowed. The brothers Kirke commenced a siege of the peaceful city.

The Kirkes were not cutthroat pirates. Given the nature of the continual if not constant struggles between England and France, their enthusiasm to seize the French settlement is understandable. From the earliest claims in the New World, there was contention among the claimants. The crown of France granted in 1622 to Pierre du Gua, Sieur de Monts, a grant of land between the fortieth and forty-sixth degree latitude, approximately from present-day New Jersey to Cape Breton

Island. England, on the other hand, claimed the territory between the Merrimack (Massachusetts) and Kennebec (Maine) rivers in the same year, and later expanded the claim to the Penobscot River. There was quite a bit of overlap and fuel for argument.

Claiming boundaries by natural features such as great rivers was used as a convenient alternative to latitudes as derived by astrolabe calculations, which could vary by instrument and the skill of the user. The Kennebec River continued to be the front line in the French and Indian Wars until the mid eighteenth century.

The Kennebec was also a dividing line for Native American settlements. Champlain noted in his journals that west of the river lived the Armouchiquois. East of the Kennebec to the St. John River were the Etchemins, now known as the Maliseet and Passamaquoddy. (Baker 136)

A French settlement such as Quebec was so close to English-occupied Newfoundland that it was too great a temptation to the brothers Kirke. Their ships blocked all trade and communication with France. Their plan was that if Champlain and his companions would not surrender, the Kirkes would starve them out. Continually watched by Kirke's crew, the people of Quebec could not venture far or often from the protection of the post buildings. Though strictly rationed, their food supplies were eventually reduced to an allotment of a few peas per person a day. At that point, Champlain decided to seek negotiations rather than have everyone die of starvation. He was unsure of how he and his terms would be received.

"We had every kind of courtesy from the English," Champlain wrote in his report. He granted that Louis Kirke was so "French in disposition" that Champlain recommended that the Hebert family and others of the families who had settled in Quebec accept Kirke's invitation to stay and continue to farm their land. The Heberts did stay as they had nothing left to return to in France. Others, who had made the crossing more recently, left, receiving nothing for their investment of money and energy. The 36 livres that each had paid at embarkation from France — about a tenth of an average worker's annual earnings — had bought them adventure and hardship and stories to tell to those who would listen. (Morison 196, 202)

That French disposition of the Kirke brothers that won the appreciation of Champlain has been attributed to their mother, who was a Frenchwoman from Dieppe. And the Kirke brothers, David, Louis, and Thomas, weren't English at all, though they had residences in London. Their father was a Scot. (Morison 191)

The Kirkes felt they could be beneficent to the French families not only because of the good manners taught to them by their mother but because the meager settlement posed no real threat to their claim for England. While the English settlement farther south in Virginia had 2,000 people actively engaged in expansion and fur trade of their own, and New England had a population of 310, New Holland, 200, and even the rocky New Foundland had 100 inhabitants, Quebec, France's leading establishment in New France, had only 72 people in 1627. The controlling hand of the Company of Merchants had been heavy. (Trudel 165)

The decision by the widow Hebert and the Couillard family to stay proved to be a good one. By 1632, through the patient efforts of Champlain, there was resolution between France and England over the unlawful seizure of Quebec by the Kirkes. As soon as the ink on the Treaty of St. Germain-en-Laye was dry, Louis XIII sent Champlain back to Quebec. (Trudel 175)

The brothers Kirke were not forgotten. David was knighted by the English King in 1633 and Lewis in 1643. All three became naturalized citizens of England in 1639. Their adventure in Quebec had brought them fame and, for a time, fortune. They had been cocky enough to name their illegal venture in fur trading and seizure of Quebec the Company of Adventurers to Canada. Their short sojourn to the New World had paid off well.

Conversion, not Commerce

Not every passenger aboard a ship heading west was after fame and fortune. Among the earliest travelers to Quebec was the Jesuit Paul Le Jeune of the Society of Jesus. As superior to the missions in Canada, he was required to write detailed reports to the provincial general in France. After enduring the hardships of the three-month voyage, his first report made the admission, "It is one thing to reflect upon the death in one's (monastery) cell, before the image on the Crucifix, but it is quite another to think of it in the midst of a tempest and in the presence of death itself." (Mealing 16)

Le Jeune was happy to arrive. "On Thursday, June 3rd (1632)," he wrote, "we passed into the country through one of the most beautiful rivers in the world. The great Island of Newfoundland intercepts it at its mouth, leaving two openings whereby it can empty into the sea. Upon entering, you discover a gulf 150 leagues (450 miles; the miles-to-leagues ratio being 3:1) wide; going further up, where this grand river begins to narrow, it is even there 37 leagues wide. Where we are, in Quebec, distant over 200 leagues from its mouth, it is still half a league wide. ..." It was this narrowing of the St. Lawrence that was given the name kebec by the native people. (Mealing 17)

The Jesuits were of a mind to save the natives from their barbarism through education, instruction, and settlement. "They are already tired of their miseries and stretch out their hands to us for help ..." Le Jeune wrote in an early report. Luckily he could leave behind Europe's dismal examples of the Spanish Inquisition, the Crusades, the inventive tortures of the Tower of London, and cruel naval discipline — examples of civilization gone awry. (Mealing 19)

Le Jeune experienced his own little torments when he first went ashore. "I thought I would be eaten up by the mosquitoes, which are little flies, troublesome in the extreme. The great forests here engender several species of them; there are common flies, gnats, fireflies, mosquitoes, large flies, and a number of others; the large flies sting furiously, and the pain from their sting lasts a long time. The gnats are very small, hardly visible, but very perceptibly felt; the fireflies do no harm; at night they look like sparks of fire, casting a greater light than the glowworms that I have seen in France. As to the mosquitoes, they are disagreeable beyond description. Some people are compelled to go to bed after coming from the woods, they are so badly stung." (Mealing 19)

Le Jeune was welcomed by Madame Hebert, the widow of Louis. She, with Champlain's counsel, had decided to stay in Quebec after it was taken by the brothers Kirke in 1629. Hers was the oldest house of Quebec and had not been burned by the English, as had other buildings. Of Hebert's family, Le Jeune wrote, "She has a fine family, and her daughter is married here to an honest Frenchman. God is blessing them every day; he has given them very beautiful children, their cattle are in fine condition, and their land produces good grain. This is the only French family settled in Canada." (Mealing 20) (The family is portrayed in Appendix IV.)

On his part, Captain Thomas Kirke, "having seen the Patents signed by the hand of his King, promised that he would go away within a week, and, in fact, he began preparations for going, although with regret; but his people were all very glad of the return of the French, for they had been given only six pounds of bread, French weight, for an entire week. They told us that the Savages had helped them to live during the greater part of the time. On the following Tuesday, the 13th of July (1632), they restored the fort to the hands of monsieur Emery de Caen and monsieur du Plessis Bochart, his Lieutenant; and on the same day set sail in the two ships they had anchored here. God knows if our French people were happy, seeing the dislodgment of these Anglicized Frenchmen, who had done so much injury to these poor countries." (Mealing 20-21)

The French began their work again. "It must be confessed," wrote Jesuit Le Jeune in his 1634 report, "that the work is great in these beginnings: the men are the horses and oxen; they carry or drag wood, trees, or stones; they till the soil, they harrow it. The insects in summer, the snows in winter, and a thousand other inconveniences, are very troublesome. The youth who in France worked in the shade find here a great difference. I am astonished that the hardships they have to undergoe, in doing things they have never done before, do not cause them to make a greater outcry that they do." (Mealing 24)

Not all stuck with it. Some hardy and enterprising young men escaped to the forests to be coureurs des bois, "runners in the woods," and ran a black market for furs as middlemen between the native hunters and whichever ship captain would pay the best price for the pelts. It was impossible for the few soldiers sent to Quebec to patrol such a vast expanse of land and countless bays and inlets where a ship's sloop could land. Unofficial trading was rampant, which made the monopoly granted the mercantile companies nearly worthless. In addition to having to make a profit to stay in the competition, the companies were obliged to supply the trading fort and pay its employees. Economically, Sully was right. An unenforceable monopoly in a far away, difficult climate made no economic sense — or centimes.

As for the "minor duties of the house," Le Jeune described these as "cooking, baking, making shoes, making clothes, looking after the garden, ... washing, tinkering, caring for the cattle, the milk, the butter, etc." He estimated that it would take "three good Brothers" to do all that for the Jesuit's rectory. The women of Quebec were expected to do all of that and whatever "minor duties" child rearing would entail as well, each in her own household.

Could Always be Worse

To put all into perspective, the natives had it even worse. In another 1634 account by Le Jeune, titled "What one must suffer in wintering with the savages," he compares a native's house to a prison: "This prison, in addition to the uncomfortable position that one must occupy upon a bed of earth, has four other great discomforts, — cold, heat, smoke, and dogs. As to the cold, you have the snow at your head with only a pine branch between, often with nothing but your hat, and the winds are free to enter at a thousand places. For do not imagine that these pieces of bark (covering a frame of sapling poles) are joined as paper is glued and fitted to a window frame; even if there were only the opening at the top, which serves at once as window and chimney, the coldest winter in France could come in there every day without any trouble. When I lay down at night I could study through this opening both the Stars and the Moon as easily as if I had been in the open fields.

"Noevertheless the cold did not annoy me as much as the heat from the fire. A little place like their cabins is easily heated by a good fire, which sometimes roasted and broiled me on all sides, for the cabin was so narrow that I could not protect myself against the heat. You cannot move to right or left, for the Savages, your neighbors, are at your elbows; you cannot withdraw to the rear, for you encounter the wall of snow (the cabin poles are place atop a four-foot wall of snow, not in the ground), or the bark of the cabin which shuts you in. I did not know what position to take. Had I stretched myself out, the place was so narrow that my legs would have been half way in the fire; to roll myself up in a ball, and crouch down that way, was a position I could not retain as long as they could; my clothes were all scorched and burned. You will ask me perhaps if the snow at our backs did not melt under so much heat. I answer, 'no'; that if sometimes the heat softened it in the least, the cold immediately turned it into ice. I will say, however, that both the cold and the heat are endurable, and that some remedy may be found for these two evils.

"But as to the smoke, I confess to you that it is martyrdom. It almost killed me, and made me weep continually, though I had neither grief nor sadness in my heart. It sometimes grounded all of us who were in the cabin; that is, it caused us to place our mouths against the earth in order to breathe; as it were to eat the earth, so as not to eat the smoke. I have sometimes remained several hours in that position, especially during the most severe cold and when it snowed; for it was then the smoke assailed us with the greatest fury." (Mealing 32-33)

The staunchness of the natives amazed the missionaries who came to spread their own style of fortitude, and at times the natives put the missionaries to shame. Jesuit Jean de Brebeuf cautioned the administrators back home in France not to send complainers to work in the missions. He warns newcomers that if they can't be cheerful, at least be quiet so as not to lose the respect of the people. "What shall I say of their strange patience in poverty, famine and sickness?" Brebeuf wrote in May 1635. "We have seen this year whole villages prostrated, their food a little insipid sagamite (which was said to taste like wallpaper paste); and yet not a word of complaint, not a movement of impatience. They receive indeed the news of death with more constancy that those of Christian Gentlemen and Ladies to whom one would not dare to mention it." (Mealing 46, 49, 154)

Neighboring Acadia

In 1632 Louis XIII sent Isaac de Razilly to Acadia with a contingent of 300 soldiers, laborers, and craftsmen to reclaim that portion of New France. Throughout the venture in the New World, Canada and Acadia were treated separately, although together they formed New France. For both of them, the next turning point would be 1759. There would be no return.

Royal Interests

Samuel de Champlain died on Christmas Day, December 25, 1635. His passing was much mourned.

The colony slumbered on. The permanent population established by the original eighteen families (see Appendix IV) was bolstered occasionally by groups sent out by seigniors, who made weak attempts to fulfill their contract of 300 emigrants annually. Joining them were the Filles de Roi (daughters of the king), a group of ladies from Paris and the provinces who were provided with land, supplies, a dowry of 20 livres, and a chance of finding a husband and a new life in New France. The debate of whether or not they were ladies of the night or just women without means or family has yet to bring a verdict. Courts of the era often did send prostitutes to convents for reformation or gentle incarceration instead of to jail, but no evidence of deportation of demoiselles has come to light.

Soon after Louis XIV came of age there were dark, dangerous days in France. Civil war, called the Frondes for the slingshots used to through stones through the windows of houses of the wealthy, raged from 1648 to 1651. Wandering gangs stole and slaughtered livestock. Farmers were either too afraid to work the fields or too poor to buy what they needed to farm. Weeds and brambles choked the land, which was so expensive that a common laborer would need a century's worth of wages to buy a lot large enough to support a family. The royal granaries had to provide relief to the starving in rural villages, and the government was forced to import food from foreign countries, such as Poland — a huge blow to the French national ego, such as it was. Paris itself was terrorized by thieves and murderers.

Then, in 1661, Jean-Baptiste Colbert came on the scene. He became advisor to Louis XIV. Together they schemed ...

Colbert, an industrialist, pulled France up by the bootstraps. Louis XIV had in Colbert the shoehorn to do it. "Never forget that it is by work that a king rules," said the king himself.

Through regulation and enticement, Colbert brought about a renaissance of business. Ships were built, mines dug, foundries and mills constructed, and a textile trade established to support Savonnerie carpets and Gobelin tapestries. (Horne 142, 152)

The king and his counselor Colbert took over the reins of development of New France from the mercantile Company of One Hundred Associates in 1663 and appointed Jean Talon as first intendant and Gilles Rageot as first notary to the king's court in Quebec in 1666. France was on the road to recovery. (Vachon 18)

The establishment of direct involvement by the king was the first indication that France was finally taking New France seriously. The intendant was charged with supervising the administration of finance and justice and the enforcement of law. Royal notaries were nominated by the king or his representative, such as the governor or intendant, and could practice any place covered by his commission. Seigneury notaries were assigned to the lands of that legal unit. The records of the clerks of the court of New France are priceless sources of information about the inhabitants, their occupations, marriages, death, and descendants. (Chartrand 2) (Durant 384)

The duties of a notary varied as to the time and region they served. During the seventeenth century in Canada, notaries maintained the correspondence between Quebec and Paris. They wrote and recorded land transactions, marriage contracts, wills, the disposition of property, settlement of debts, and even the census of the population. A notary, while plying his craft, was an intricate part of the orderly workings of society. But most notaries also had other occupations, ranging from surveyor to physician, because the pay for a notary was meager. No lawyers were permitted to practice in New France, but notaries were allowed to represent clients before a tribunal. Procedures were limited, and an acceptable compromise was the goal. This was done to keep the judicial system simple, fast, and inexpensive. A wise goal, given the intricacies and delays of European courts and the small, interactive population in Canada. (Vachon 40-41, 44)

Gilles Rageot, the first notary named for Canada directly by the king, handled the transfer of the property of the last mercantile company in New France to the king's government in 1675. Rageot previously had been the notary in the jurisdiction of Quebec. He also served as clerk of the court for the Prevote de Quebec. (Chartrand 23)

Three of Rageot's sons became notaries. Charles Rageot de Saint-Luc succeeded his father and became clerk of the court of the Prevote de Quebec in 1693 and was a royal notary from 1695 to 1702, when he died at age thirty. His brother Nicolas Rageot de Saint-Luc was named clerk of the court of the Prevote de Quebec and royal notary March 15, 1703, but he died sixteen days later, on March 31, 1703. If three's the charm, then Francois Rageot de Beaurivage, the third son was the beneficiary. Intendant Jacques Raudot named Francois as royal notary to Quebec in 1711. Francois served the courts for forty years and retired in 1752 to Saint-Thomas, where he died in 1754. (Chartrand 30-32, 36)

In 1665, the Carignan-Salieres Regiment, France's first standing army unit, was sent to Canada to subdue the Mohawks, an Iroquois tribe, which used guerrilla tactics of attack and then blended into the forest. The troops were seasoned, having fought

the Turks in 1659, and were offered land if they stayed in
Quebec when their enlistment were up. This added about 400
able-bodied men to the population. (Judd 88)

Chapter Three

Looking Back

If Henry IV's Sully had taken a greater interest in exploration and empire expansion, the settlers of Quebec would probably have received, in addition to funding, more regulation and more intrusion into their lifestyle and a very different culture would have resulted. As it were, benign neglect allowed the formulation of an open, "laid back" society that knew the worth of team effort and hard work but also the value of enjoying the good weather when it came, good neighbors when help was needed, fine feasting when there was enough food, and the call of the great outdoors.

A 1712 report by Gedeon de Catalogne, an engineer, shows the writer's exasperation with the new Canadian attitude. He wrote, "the settlers seemed to be always ready to leave their farms and betake themselves to the forests," blaming the "seductive charm of the fur traffic."

Catalogne was right. Even in Quebec's earliest days, the freedom of the woods beckoned. Noel Langlois, who arrived before 1634 and worked as a carpenter, turned to the life of hunting and fishing after he was granted the seigniory (a large section of land for subleasing and development) of Port Joli in 1677. He had some work done to develop the land for farming and grazing, but not enough to sustain himself and his family. In a few years' time, they were at the mercy of the colony for subsistence. (Munro 51)

The Homestead

Even families with land allotments much smaller than a seigniory had their stand of woods. The typical habitant lot ran from the St. Lawrence River north 40 to 80 arpents and was 10 to 20 arpents wide, but that was soon reduced to 3 or 4 arpents wide. (An arpent is about 65 meters, or approximately 215 feet.)

Rows of lots, collectively called a rang, fronted the St. Lawrence River, which was the only means of transportation for nearly a century. The lots were angled northwest by southwest from the river and were surveyed. The surveyors often put bits of crockery or glass — items that only Europeans had at that time — under a pile of stones to mark the boundaries. Surveyors often used a quadrant or astrolabe at 9 or 10 a.m. or noon to fix the lot lines.

The waterfront of a rang was called the fronteau or devanture. The rear boundary was often a natural feature such as another river or sharp precipice. Eventually the length of a rang was set uniformly at one mile. The straight line that formed at the rear of the first rang became the edge of the road that was built along it when all the river rangs had been settled by the early eighteenth century.

The road cleared between the first and second rangs was called a fronteau, even though it was a mile away from the water. It was the fronteau of the second rang that introduced a new method of transportation — long distance movement by foot, horse, cart, or sleigh. But with the new convenience came more responsibility. Each habitant, or settler, was responsible to clear and maintain the road that fronted his lot. In the winter this meant bringing out the plow after each significant snow storm.

The second rang was laid out parallel to the river. Families often purchased a lot just across the road from their original lot and gave it their children or grandchildren to keep the family close by. The original farm house, built beside the river, was often hauled along the length of the lot to a new location to face the road. The move was usually done during the winter when the ground was frozen and the structure could be moved on logs used as rollers. Sometimes the terrain of the long, narrow lots were too rough, too full of marshes and rock outcroppings, to allow a building to roll across. In that case, the old house was abandoned or dismantled and a new one constructed near the road. (Rioux 6-7)

The varied terrain within a long narrow lot was just one of the inconveniences of the layout selected for the rangs. A self-sufficient farm a mile in length made cattle raising a time-consuming chore. The cows had to be led out to a meadow, which was usually remote from the barn, and had to be driven back twice a day for milking. In rainy weather, the mud made the coming and going difficult. The same was true for wood cutting. Close at hand at the start of settlement, the stand of wood gradually receded away from the house as the land was cleared for garden and pasture. To compensate, much of the wood was cut during the winter and brought to the homestead by sled.

As settlement expanded from Quebec west to Montreal, the river and the subsequently constructed road became one long main street, often called the longest one in North America, with the homes of families strung along it on the long and narrow parallel strip lots. The closeness of neighbors served a twofold purpose in early Quebec. In addition to making maintenance of the road less burdensome, the neighbors were within shouting distance should there be an emergency such as a sudden attack by enemy tribes of natives or an accident while working with ax or plow, fire or cauldron, or during childbirth. Neighbors were also close at hand for social interaction. The "premier voisin," as the closest neighbor was called, played an important role. That was the individual who was called to for help, consulted for advice, invited to all celebrations, and given a share of a good day of bread baking or a portion from a successful hunt.

The habitants adapted the once-hated "corvee" to their own use. In France, the corvee was a form of tax collected through physical labor performed by tenants for the landlord in lieu of paying the tax in hard currency. In Quebec, the corvee took the form of clearing and maintaining the road along the seigniory, which was for everyone's mutual benefit. The corvee also became the name of neighborhood gatherings to raise or move a house, harvest a crop, clear a section of land, or spin the wool sheared from a flock of sheep.

The proximity of someone who could be counted on in any time of need or emergency was psychologically very important for the few hardy souls who braved the New World — cold, strange, and sometimes hostile as it was — and stayed to make a livelihood and, in time, a heritage for future generations in which the concept of the importance of neighbor and neighborhood, just as much as family, was strong. (Munro xli) (Rioux 10, 12)

The equality of land apportionment promoted a sense of social equality among the settlers of Quebec. There were no great lords of vast estates. Even the seigniories, though a league square, were subdivided into the traditional rang arrangement. The settlers, called censitaires, paid rent and dues, called cens et rentes, to the seignior. They usually earned the money from woodcutting or hunting. In the 1660s, the annual payment was about 20 sols per arpent of frontage and some food, such as poultry, butter or ham. The renters could use the land as they wanted with the exception of any unusually fine oak trees, which were reserved for the king's navy.

On the seignior's part, he had to build and maintain a mill to grind the settler's grain and an oven for baking bread made from the flour ground from the grain. In 1683 there were eighty-three such seigniories. The arrangement was considered so satisfactory that after Quebec came under the rule of England in 1763, censitaires continued payments of cens to the then-deposed seignior. (Rioux 5, 17) (Munro 155)

Towns were slow to develop because of the strong self-sufficiency of the habitant families on their farms. When the population of what was considered a neighborhood grew to a size large enough to support a parish priest, a lot was purchased for a church and an adjoining cemetery. The extra land within the lot was subdivided into small plots called "emplacements" and sold to older couples who had deeded their farm to a family member. The couple was referred to as "emplacitaires," and all their needs were provided for by their relatives, usually the ones who had been deeded the family homestead.

When professional people such as doctors and notaries wanted to move to town but did not want to farm, they were allowed to purchase emplacements as well. In this way the center of town was established around the parish church and service providers who lived nearby.

In Conclusion

The pioneers of New France settled a new land and set in motion a new culture. Historians have the unusual opportunity to observe the start and development of a unique society from its incubation through metamorphosis into a new nation, one that is still struggling with its national identity. One hundred and fifty years of history, 1608 to 1759, is the chrysalis from which emerges the heritage of the French Canadian and its descendant, the Francadian-American.

In 2008, Quebec, designated a World Heritage City by UNESCO in 1985, held ceremonies and hosted celebrations to commemorate 400 years of endurance. Millions of Americans of French-Canadian heritage will have had the opportunity to acknowledge and celebrate their heritage and ancestry at the 400th anniversary of the founding of Quebec by Samuel de Champlain and his men. The descendants of those hardy pioneers now can link with the history those first families of Quebec through this guide to the companions of Champlain.

REFERENCES

Baker, Emerson W., editor. *American Beginnings: Exploration, Culture, and Cartography in the Land of Norumbega.* Lincoln: University of Nebraska Press, 1994, 136.

Biggar, H.P., editor, *The Works of Samuel de Champlain*, 6 volumes. Toronto: The Champlain Society, 1925, II: 24-25, 35-36, 60-61, 345.
The six-volume compilation of Champlain's writings contains numerous illustrations and maps that were reproduced from the originals or close copies. This edition gives both the French and English translation of Champlain's reports and written works about voyages of 1603 to 1632. Only 550 copies of Biggar's work were printed for distribution to members and subscribing libraries, with 600 copies subsequently printed for sale to the general public. Copy 478 from the Fogler Library in Orono at the University of Maine was consulted.

Canadian Museum of Civilization, online <http://www.civilization.ca/treasors/treasure/222eng.html>, downloaded 1 October 2005.
The Canadian museum provides online viewing of some of its most precious artifacts, including the astrolabe attributed to Champlain. The site maintains the extensive "Dictionary of Canadian Biography Online," searchable by historical periods or by individual.

Chartrand, Rene. editor, *Early Notaries of Canada.* New Orleans: Polyanthos Inc., 1977, 30-32, 36
The introduction, written in English, provides basic instruction in the types and duties of notaries in New France. The text, written in French, also describes the work of notaries from the earliest years in Quebec to the mid eighteenth century. All known notaries are identified, and their works are listed or summarized.

Dugard, Martin. *The Last Voyage of Columbus* Boston: Little, Brown and Company, 2005, 23-24, 116, Map 3. Dugard's work helps the reader understand the rough practicalities of life at sea in the sixteenth century.

Durant, Will, and Ariel Durant. *The Age of Reason Begins: A History of European Civilization in the Period of Shakespeare, Bacon, Montaigne, Rembrandt, Galileo, and Descartes: 1558-1648.* New York: Simon and Schuster, 1961, 384.
The overleaf of this edition displays a clear map of France circa 1600. The provinces that peopled New France are in the northwest, from Saintonage to Picardy. The Durants have produced a multi-volume history of world civilization that is written so creatively that it helps present-day readers relate to past events, great and small.

Fagan, Brian. *The Little Ice Age: How Climate Made History 1300-1850.* New York: Basic Books, 2000, 51, 103.
Food is a strong motivator, and the effects of climate change on food production also effects change in economics and politics.

Fletcher, Nichola. *Charlemagne's Tablecloth: A Piquant History of Feasting.* New York: St. Martin's Press, 2004, 51, 93.
This winner of a silver medal at the Gourmet Voice Awards brings to life the tastes of the great and the small of medieval times and the Renaissance.

Greengrass, Mark. *France in the Age of Henri IV: the struggle for stability.* New York: Longman Publishing, 1995, second edition, 175-177, 296, Map 3.
"This book was intended to provide a revision of historical perspective." (ix) Not a biography of Henry IV, his reign (1589-1610) is well documented and explored. There is a 23-page bibliography of primary and secondary sources.

Gurney, Alan. *Compass: A Story of Exploration and Innovation.*
New York: W.W. Norton & Co., 2004, 24-25.
The compass is a basic tool of land and sea navigation that is
often taken for granted but which took centuries, from the
twelfth to the twentieth, to perfect. Extensive bibliography.

Horne, Alistair. *La belle France: A Short History.* New York:
Alfred A. Knopf, 2005, 109 -122, 142, 152.
Horne was awarded the French Legion d'Honneur in 1993 and
British knighthood in 2003 "for his work on French history,"
as reported on the book jacket of this American edition. This
is a valuable resource for those who do not read French yet
want an evenhanded discussion of French history.

Jette, Rene. *Dictionnaire genealogique des familles du Quebec
des origines a 1730.* Montreal: Les Presses de l'Universite de
Montreal, 1983.
This renown compilation of genealogical data includes the
work of Tanguay, Canadian census returns, church registers
and other sources.

Judd, Richard W., editor, *Maine: The Pine Tree State from
Prehistory to the Present.* Orono: University of Maine Press,
1995, 88.
The in and outs and interplay of relations and war among
Native Americans, French, and English are woven throughout
this comprehensive history.

Lanctot, Gustave. *A History of Canada*, Jospehine Hambleton,
translator. Toronto: Clark, Irwin & Co. Ltd, 1963, I: 15-16,
76, 102-103, 110, 119, 122-123, 126.
An excellent, detailed yet entertaining text and translation that
introduces Canada from its origins to the Royal Regime, 1663.

Lescarbot, Marc. *Nova Francia.* Norwood, N.J.: Theatrum Orbis
Terrarum Ltd., 1977, 91.
First published in London in 1609, this English translation of
Nova Francia by P. Erondelle from a French manuscript was

commissioned by M. Richard Hackluyt.

Mealing, S.R., editor, *The Jesuit Relations and Allied Documents, A Selection*. Toronto: Macmillan Company of Canada Limited, 1978, viii,16-17, 19, 20-21, 24, 32-33, 46, 49, 154.
This volume is a translation of a primary source, a contemporary account of early life in Quebec, that was first published in France from 1632 to 1673 and reprinted in 1868 by the government of Canada. A 73-volume edition, edited by Reuben Gold Thwaites, was published by Burrows Brothers Co. of Cleveland, Ohio, from 1896 to 1901. A selection by Edna Kenton from Thwaites' edition was published by Albert and Charles Boni, New York, in 1925. This edition was published in association with the Institute of Canadian Studies at Carleton University, Ottawa, and offers an excellent summary of historical events and background information in Mealing's introduction.

Morison, Samuel Eliot. *Samuel de Champlain, Father of New France*. Boston: Atlantic Monthly Press; Little, Brown & Co., 1972, 102, 188, 202, 237, 244.
Morison's work is respected as a basic text on Champlain and his era.

Munro, William Bennett. *Documents Relating to the Seigniorial Tenure in Canada 1598-1854*. New York: Greenwood Press, 1968, xli, 51, 155.
Originally published by the Champlain Society in 1908, the volume is a reproduction of original documents, most in French, with extensive footnotes in English. The work cites original documents and reliable sources.

Rioux, Marcel, and Yves Martin, editors, *French Canadian Society*. Toronto: McClelland and Stewart Limited, 1969, 5-7, 10, 12, 17

In this collection of essays on the social structure of early and contemporary French Canada, the "rang" system of land division, the parish and social groups of family and neighborhoods are discussed. Urban studies, language, and labor issues are also covered.

Tanguay, Cyprien. *Dictionnaire genealogique des familles canadiennes depuis la fondation de la colone jusqu 'a nos jours.* Montreal: Editions Elyssee, 1991.
The first volume of Tanguay's work covers the early years of Quebec, to approximately the year 1700. The six subsequent volumes extend the genealogies to about 1800.

Tanguay, Cyprien. *A Travers les Registres.* Montreal: Cadeau & Derome, 1886, 8.
Tanguay was a cleric who compiled a comprehensive genealogical dictionary of French-Canadian families. His work is extensively quoted in family histories and genealogy.

Trudel, Marcel. *The Beginnings of New France 1524-1663,* Patricia Claxton, translator. Canadian Centenary Series, McClelleand and Stewart Limited, 1973, 48, 124, 134, 139, 152-153, 160, 175.
Comprehensive yet not pompous nor ponderous, this summary of Champlain's own writings also draws upon rare and fragmented original sources to 1627 and the widely accepted historians H.P. Biggar, Morris Bishop, Gustave Lanctot, Mark Lescarbot, and Samuel Morison to assemble a history of New France unequaled by any other to date. This edition contains three books by Trudel: *Les vaines tentatives 1524-1603, Le comptoir 1604-27,* and *La seigneurie des Cent-Associes 1627-1663,* which in turn portray a summary of Champlain's own *Voyages* and a detailed history of fur trade monopolies and its troubles.

Vachon, Andre. *Histoire du notariat canadien.* Quebec: Les Presses de l'Universite Laval, 1962. 18, 40-41, 44.

The first of three parts deals with the organization of the notarial profession in Canada from 1621 to 1791. Written in French, this report is properly footnoted and has an extensive bibliography of manuscripts, specialized studies, and general works.

White Oak Society, Inc.,
<http://www.whiteoak.org/learning/timeline.htm> updated 13 July 2001.
The fur trade timeline on this site is chronological and offers a progressive view of the development and final downfall of the North American industry.

Wilford, John Noble. *The Mapmakers: The Story of the Great Pioneers in Cartography from Antiquity to the Space Age.* New York, Vintage Books, 1982, 94-95, 98.
With the precision of a mathematician and the skill of a good storyteller, Wilford develops his tale chronologically, from early mapmakers to extraterrestrial exploration — the moon and Mars. Part 2 surveys the sixteenth and seventeenth centuries.

Though not referred to in the text, the following might be of interest to family historians and genealogists.

Careless, J.M.S. editor. *The Pioneers. An Illustrated History of Early Settlement in Canada.* Toronto: McClelland and Stewart Limited, 1973.
J.M.S. Careless, a professor of History at the University of Toronto, wrote the introduction. The volume is one of the Canadian Illustrated Library publications.

Azarie Couillard-Despres, *Louis Hebert: premier colon Canadien et sa famille.* Montreal: Institution des Sourds-muets, 1918.
Written by an abbot who was a descendant of Louis Herbert, the book first was published in 1906 as *La premiere famille*

francaise au Canada as a commemorative of the 300th
anniversary of Quebec. A retelling of the history of New
France, the author used the writings of Champlain and Lanctot
and the works of Tanguay.

C.M. Day (Mrs.), *Pioneers of the Eastern Townships*. Milton,
Canada: Global Heritage Press, 2000.
Originally published in 1863 by John Lovell, Montreal, it is "a
work containing official and reliable information respecting
the formation of settlements; with incidents in their early
history; and details of adventures, perils and deliverances." —
introduction.
The book is also a record of English settlers "taking up land"
and making it their own. Descriptions of the land grants,
travel conditions, and primitive housing is applicable of life
throughout northeastern North America during the late
eighteenth and early nineteenth centuries.

Rudy and Joy Favretti, *For Every House a Garden: A Guide to
Reproducing Period Gardens*. Hanover, N.H.: University
Press of New England, 1990.
Family historians who would like to recreate gardens
reminiscent of those of early Quebec can consult this guide as
to layout and plant lists. The text gives the historical
background of gardens from 1607 to 1900, from medieval
gardens, with designs similar to the one sketched by
Champlain for l'Habitation, to gardens of craftsmen and
workmen of the nineteenth century. There are extensive lists
of plants that are authentic to designated time periods.

Allan Greer, *Peasant, Lord, and Merchant: Rural Society in
Three Quebec Parishes 1740-1840*. Toronto, University of
Toronto Press, 1985.
A scholarly study of habitant culture.

William Manchester, *A World Lit Only by Fire: The Medieval
Mind and the Renaissance —Portrait of an Age*. Boston:
Little, Brown and Company, Back Bay Books, 1993.

The sixteenth century built the stage for the New World
explorations and settlements in the seventeenth century.
Manchester, in a straightforward way, introduces the social
and economic reasons behind well-known but often poorly
understood historical events. Included in the text are
descriptions of the methods used to arrive at the educated
guess.

Dava Sobel, *Galileo's Daughter*. New York: Walker & Co.,
    1999.
    The story of an extraordinary man sets the stage for great
    leaps of science at the turn of the sixteenth to seventeenth
    centuries.

Marcel Trudel, *Introduction to New France*. Pawtucket, R.I.:
    Quintin Publications, 1997.
    This is a reprint of the Holt, Rinehart and Winston of Canada
    Limited original publication. It gives a good overview of the
    difficulties encountered when settling Quebec and touches on
    the settlement of Montreal and Acadia.

Map of Northeastern North America

Saguenay · Tadoussac · St. Lawrence River · Gaspé · Gaspésie · Atlantic Ocean · Quebec · New Brunswick · St. John · Maine · Kennebec · Penobscot · St. Croix Island · Port Royal · Nova Scotia · N.H. · Mass. · R.I. · Atlantic Ocean

Drawn from maps provided by National Park Service

APPENDIX I

The Method of French-Canadian Genealogical Research.
An Opportunity of a lifetime

The historical situation of French Canada is unique. Settlement of the population from European origin does not stretch back into prehistory. The time period is finite — 1608 to 1763 — from the founding of Quebec and the commencement of French emigration to the concession of Canada to England and the virtual cessation of immigration to Canada from France.

During the French settlement time, the Catholic Church kept careful records of birth and baptisms, marriages, and death and burial, as is the practice of the church. The marriage records were of particular use by the parishes in an effort to avoid intermarriage among first and second cousins. Given the limited population, the physical constrictions of the province, and the social isolation of language, politics, and religion, this was a real health concern as well as a religious one. The Province of Quebec was an island of "Francadian" culture, i.e., French Canadian, and remains so to a certain degree to this day.

The two leading resources for tracing French-Canadian vital records, i.e., births, marriages, and deaths, are the genealogical dictionaries by Cyprien Tanguay and Rene Jette. Tanguay's work, "Dictionnaire genealogique des familles canadiennes depuis la fondation de la colonie jusqu'a nos jours," includes records from 1608 to 1800. Jette restricted his work, "Dictionnaire genealogique des familles du Quebec: des origines a 1730," from the 1600s to 1730 but utilized secular records as well as church ones and had the advantage of double checking Tanguay's work, which was published previous to his. J. Arthur Leboeuf published corrections to Tanguay's work in "Complement au dictionnaire genealogique Tanguay."

Other compilations and some computerized databases of French-Canadian genealogy have been developed. See *Dictionary of Canadian Biography* (DCB/DBC), Drouin, and PRDH in Appendix II.

Be wary of the Net

The Internet might facilitate research for the amateur genealogist, but there are serious dangers in relying on the information given on electronic Web pages. Nothing on the Net replaces the hard evidence of primary documents.

Internet sites should be examined before any information is taken from them. Look at the suffix of the site address. If it is ".org," then the site is run by a nonprofit organization. Government sites end in ".gov." Find the name of the author of the site and look for the person's qualifications. Be cautious of linked sites. Though the original site might be legitimate, sites that branch from it might be less so.

Any and all information gathered from the Net should be double checked with reliable sources, either primary or secondary. Misinformation can lead a genealogist down the wrong branch of a family tree or even to the wrong tree. User beware!

Start at the very beginning

On standard genealogy charts, which are known as pedigree charts, the compiler is No. 1. Though it might seem unnecessary, the compiler should request an official copy of his or her birth certificate from the city or town in which the birth took place. Upon receipt, the embossed copy should be placed in an archival quality sheet protector, photocopied, then placed in a fireproof box or other secure container. The photocopy is the working copy and should be put in a binder or file for easy reference.

Even a person's own birth certificate can bring surprises. A man by the name of Bob was not amused when he returned home from his visit to the draft board in the 1940s. His parents had never told him that legally his first name was Phillip. Family members had always called him Robert or Bob. At birth, he was named Phillip to honor a friend of his father, but after a falling out, little Phillip was called by his middle name, Robert. No one had discussed the subject until that day at the draft board. Bob now signs his name as P. Robert.

Request copies of parents' marriage certificate and birth certificates and those of grandparents, as well as any death certificates. Continue the process for great-grandparents and so on, using the information in each certificate to help find the earlier ones. The goal is to collect birth, marriage, and death certificates or records for all direct ancestors back to the generations covered by Jette and Tanguay. From that point, the information can be taken from these two reliable sources. The final step is to request copies of official documents from local, state, or federal offices or the National Archives of Canada. Large agencies need the names of the individuals and the exact dates of the event. Clerks of small towns often are obliging about searching town ledgers if enough information is given.

Family address books and albums can give birth dates and previous addresses. Legal documents such as deeds, probate records, and wills can provide good clues. Draw from each record whatever information can lead to a vital record.

Identifying all the blood-related members of a family is a daunting task but can be the basis for a very rewarding hobby. Genealogy has all the challenge of a good mystery, the thrill of the chase. Putting names, dates, and locations in their proper places in the family line and in the context of history is a puzzle that has to be assembled in order to be solved. Genealogy is a game that could — and usually does — last a lifetime, taking the seeker to unknown corners of the Earth — or one's own attic.

APPENDIX II

The ABCs of French-Canadian Genealogy

A glossary of terms used in genealogy in general and French-Canadian studies in particular, including English translations of French terms that are often encountered in genealogy research.

{ A }

Acadie: The region of North America claimed by the French. At first, Acadie ranged from the 40th to the 46th degrees of latitude, but later came to be considered what is now Nova Scotia and part of New Brunswick. Permanent settlement of Acadia, as it came to be called, started in 1636, with the arrival of several families from France.

l'acte de deces: death certificate

Archives nationales du Quebec: www.anq.gouv.qc.ca
There are nine branches of the National Archives, each holding the records of its region, with some overlap. If the archives does not hold the records that are requested, the archivist will usually tell the inquirer which branch has them. Branches are located in Rimouski (lower St. Lawrence and Gaspesie), Chicoutimi (Saguenay and Lac St. Jean), Sainte-Foy (Quebec City), Trois Rivieres (Mauricie and central Quebec), Sherbrooke, Montreal, Hull, Rouyn-Noranda (Abitibi-Temiscamingue and northern Quebec), and Sept-Illes (north coast). Full addresses are available on the Web site.
The archives of Canada have joined forces with the national library to offer services to the public. The central office is in Ottawa. The Web site can be reached through www.archives.ca and www.collectionscanada.ca/index-e.html. On the Web site are the Canadian Genealogy Center, which offers "Tracing Your Ancestors in Canada"; databases of sources of records and societies and 800 archival institutions; and directions on how to request copies of records. There are many

links to Canadian resources, including the "Dictionary of Canadian Biography Online."

arpent: In Quebec, an arpent of land was a little less than an acre, about .84 acre.

arpenteur: surveyor

avis: notice

{ B }

Banal rights, i.e., banalites: A French feudal practice that in Quebec came to be understood as the obligation of a seignior to provide a grist mill for the milling of grain by the renters. The renters in turn gave grain or baked bread to the grant holder.

benevole: volunteer

briquetier: brickmaker

{ C }

Canada: The name most likely originated from the Huron-Iroquois word "kanata," which means "village" or "community." Jacques Cartier used the name in reference to Stadacona, which stood where Quebec was founded by Champlain and his men in 1608. Canada was considered separate from Acadie, both being lands in New France. The name became official by the Constitutional Act of 1791, with the areas of Lower Canada, which included Quebec, and Upper Canada, referring to the "River of Canada," the St. Lawrence. The Dominion of Canada was formed in 1867 by the British North America Act. New Brunswick and Nova Scotia joined the province of Canada, which included Ontario and Quebec. Manitoba joined the federation in 1870; British Columbia in 1871; Prince Edward Island in 1873; Alberta and Saskatchewan in 1905; and Newfoundland in 1949.

Carignan-Salieres Regiment: The regiment was the only unit of regular troops to be sent from France. Its mission was to protect Quebec and subdue the Iroquois. Of the 1,000 men, about 400 remained in Canada after serving for three years, from 1665 to 1668.

Census:

The first Canadian census was taken in 1666 and showed a population of 3,215. The estimated population of people of French extraction in Canada in 1763 was 70,000. Immigration to Canada from France has been estimated at 10,000.

Microfilm of Canadian censuses through 1901 are available through interlibrary loan with the help of participating libraries. Major libraries and those with genealogical collections often have microfilm of U.S. census records from 1790 through 1930, with the exception of 1890, which was destroyed by a fire in 1921. The 1850 U.S. census was the first one to list all members of a household.

Census data is considered secondary source material. Accuracy of information in a census varies widely and depends on the reliability of the person who responded to the census taker.

Certified copies of documents: These cost time and money and should be carefully preserved:

— As soon as it is received, place the certified copy in an archival-quality sheet protector.

— Photocopy the certified copy through the protector. Don't take it out.

— Store the protected certified copy in a fireproof box.

— Use the photocopy for analysis and as a work sheet. Circle differences of spelling, dates, etc. Underline information that is useful.

charron: wheelwright; a charron in early Quebec would make the wheels for the cannon that were used for defense against the Iroquois and enemies from Europe.

chirurgien: surgeon

Citations — Citing sources:
For every note and quote, write the source citation. Cite every source.

The first time a source document is used, write the citation out in full: author's full name, book's full title, city of publication, name of publisher, date published. Then add the page number whenever a citation, the information or quotation, is used. For subsequent citations, write only the author's last name and the page numbers. If more than one source by the same author is used, add a key word from the title between the author's name and the page numbers.

Genealogists have the responsibility of ferreting out the truth and culling out false statements. The source book *Evidence! Citation & Analysis for the Family Historian* by Elizabeth Shown Mills, published by Genealogical Publishing Company, Baltimore, 1997, is a guide for the genealogist to stay on the straight and narrow of solid research. It is a manual for writing a citation for every scrap of information that might go into a family history and genealogy. Mills also prompts the researcher to ask important questions as to whether or not the author of a source is reliable, whether or not sources are identified, and how close to the original document or actual event is the information given.

If sources do not agree and there are conflicting names or dates, cite each source; e.g., for birth records, give the information from each record: b(1), b(2), b(3), etc.

The further in time the source is from the primary source, the more suspect it is. A "fact" is correct only until it is proven incorrect by a more reliable source. Even the Bible, which has a genealogy section of its own, acknowledges how stories can seem so pausible until the truth comes to light: "Any story sounds true until someone sets the record straight." Proverbs 18:17. Don't be misled by unsubstantiated information. Ask for sources. Check them for yourself.

Civil records in Canada:
        Birth records in Canada became civil records starting in 1926. Before then, churches were required to keep baptismal, marriage, and burial records, but some record keeping was lax and others were lost. Marriage record holdings started in 1970, with churches doing the recording before then. Notary records were centralized in 1961. Records predating 1961 often require the name of the parish, the date, and the name of the district that received a copy from the church. Be warned that districts sometimes changed as to which parishes they encompassed.

Collecting data:
Minimize confusion and clutter to maximize results:
— Write out an index card for each repository or organization contacted.
— Include the name of the agency, full address, phone number, e-mail and Web site.
— List what records are available and the charge for copies.

comte: county

les coordonnees: contact information

corvee: a tax by which the seigniors of New France could call on the habitants to give three days of labor a year, for seeding, haying, and at harvest.

Conseil Souverain: The Sovereign Council of New France comprised the governor, bishop, councilors selected from leading citizens, an attorney general, and a clerk. The council, granted political and judicial powers for the administration of New France, was established by royal edict in 1663 by Louis XIV.

coureurs de bois: Men who left the settlements of New France and went to live and trade with the native people, without having obtained a license to do so, as opposed to the voyageur, who was a licensed trader.

courrier or courriel electronique: e-mail

{ D }

declaration de mort: declaration of death

dernieres voluntes: last wishes

diaspora: An involuntary movement of a large percentage of a population. The Acadian diaspora, known as the Grand Derangement, began in 1755. The English forcibly relocated approximately 7,000 people of French descent to the English colonies along the Atlantic coast, Louisiana, England, France, and other areas along the east coast of present-day Canada.

Dictionary of Canadian Biography, www.biographi.ca/EN/, is a research and publishing project of the University of Toronto and Universite Laval, begun in 1959. Is often referred to as DCB/DBC.

direct evidence: contemporary statement of names, dates, locations, and times involved in an event. Birth and marriage certificates are examples of direct evidence. A baptismal certificate is indirect evidence of a birth date if the exact date of the birth is not stated. Early French-Canadians maintained a practice of baptizing babies the day after birth, but that was not always possible. Baptism dates are often given in French-Canadian genealogies, rather than birth dates.

dit: also known as. "Dit" names were taken or given to individuals to distinguish them from others whose surname was the same or similar. Many times a location was added to a surname to identify a branch of a family. Frequently the old surname part eventually was omitted and only the "dit" part was used by a family.

dossier: file (such as on a person)

Drouin Genealogical Institute was begun in 1899 by Joseph Drouin, who was a lawyer. A trade name was awarded in 1913. Joseph's son Gabriel Drouin took on the task of microfilming the vital records of Quebec Province. There are now the "red" Drouin, the National Dictionary of French-Canadians, and the "blue" Drouin, a two-part, masculine and feminine series of marriages from 1760 to 1935.

The institute prepares reports for paying customers using pre-1960 files of completed family genealogy "cases" and post-1960 Kardex, microfilm, and data. The institute sells materials to libraries and societies. The American French Genealogical Society, the L'AFGS, has some commercial rights for use and distribution in the United States.

A genealogical project called GenWeb has offered single "look-ups" of Drouin records for free. The Web site, if still active, is: www.rootsweb.com/~canqc/lookups.htm. If no longer operational, a search for GenWeb or the shortened URL www.rootsweb.com might be of use.

{ E }

engage: hired worker with a contract

Epidemics caused many deaths during the centuries without immunizations. Here are some of those that have been recorded. The dates might come up again and again in a genealogy, showing how families were devastated by these fatal illnesses:
1616 and 1617: chicken pox in New England to the Kennebec River.
1633: small pox along the Connecticut River, New York, Maine, Quebec.
(Source: Tom Wessels, *Reading the Forested Landscape: A Natural History of New England*, (Woodstock, Vt., Countryman Press, 1997)

epouse: spouse

eveche: bishopric

{ F }

FirstGov.gov is a Web site that links to all 50 states, giving access to reliable information about how to request copies of vital records, find out about local historical societies that might be good resources, and read about an area's culture and heritage.

fils aine: eldest son

fond: file folder

Food. The sharing of a meal or a cup of tea or coffee brings together the members of a family. The food shared often takes on a special significance. Gathering the recipes used for meals can enrich a family history.

 Some classic Canadian-heritage foods include tortiere, a two-crust pie made with ground meat or flaked salmon; thick pea soup; ployes, which are buckwheat pancakes; crepes, very thin pancakes made with many eggs. From native Americans, Canadians added Brazil, i.e., kidney beans, corn, cucumbers, melons, and squash to their diet. Along the Bay of Fundy, habitants grew cabbage to feed to the cattle and pigs during the winter. There was fish enough for all, from the rivers and streams. Habitants did not have the means to fish in the ocean but did trade for deep-water fish.

Formatting a genealogy:
 Superscripts — those tiny numbers that sit on the shoulder of the last word of a referenced entry — are often difficult for the nonacademic to use. A less formidable format for the amateur genealogist is the endnote. If used consistently, endnotes can be just as useful as superscripted footnotes.
 Endnotes are often grouped by chapter. In a genealogy, endnotes could be grouped by married couple or family group. The reference number would be the ancestral number. See Appendix V.

Francadian: The author's designation for a French-Canadian or someone of French-Canadian heritage. The use of the term Franco-American appears to negate the Canadian element of the heritage. Not all Americans of French extraction have a Canadian element in their background. The uniqueness of the French colonial experiment in Canada and the resulting culture appears to merit the inclusion of the Canadian designation.

{ G }

Genealogy charts, also known as pedigree charts: Relationships displayed on genealogy charts are very precise and easily calculated. The compiler of the chart is No. 1. The parents of the compiler are Nos. 2 and 3, the male always being assigned the even numbers; the female, the odds.

greffes des notaires: office of the clerk of the court

greffier: clerk of the court

{ H }

habitant: Settler in New France; later, country folk, as compared to city dweller.

l'Habitation: Large fortified dwellings built by Champlain and his men at Port Royal in 1605 and at Quebec in 1608, which stood on the site of the present-day Notre Dame des Victoires.

l'homologation: probate

Huguenots: French Protestants who were influenced by Martin Luther and John Calvin. Huguenots were banned from entering Canada after 1633. The Edict of Nantes in 1598 gave them religious freedom, but it was revoked in 1685, at which time approximately 400,000 fled from France.

huissier: bailiff

{ I }

Immigration documentation

Looking for immigration papers in the United States, for those entering the country prior to 1906, is looking for the proverbial needle in a haystack. Any lawful court, local, county, or state, could issue naturalization papers. A federal agency took over Sept. 27, 1906.

There are two parts to naturalization, the declaration of intention and final papers. Usually the date of one or the other is required to find the court documents. Courts closest to a person's residence are the best places to start the search.

Internet. The proverb, "Oh, what a wicked web we weave when first we practice to deceive," was never so true as it is in the age of technology. Even when well intentioned, names, dates, and other information taken from a Web site can lead a genealogist down a wrong branch or even up the wrong tree. Nothing on the Internet should be taken at face value. Every "fact" should be double checked in the original document. If no source for some data is given, the information should be used only as a lead or clue, not as fact. Some researchers write suspect notes in pencil and recopy in ink only after the information is verified.

Look at the designation at the end of the URL, the Internet address. The ending .gov means the site is produced by a government agency; .org signifies a nonprofit organization; .com is a commercial site. If any Internet address does not open, use a search engine and enter the name of the organization or business as the search terms.

Government sites can provide links to local, state, and federal offices and agencies that might be able to provide documentation of a birth, marriage, death, or court action. For the United States, FirstGov.gov is an excellent resource. Maine's site is www.maine.gov.

In Maine, the Maine State Library is a treasure trove for genealogists. A listing of its holdings can be found on its Web site, www.state.me.us/msl under "Collections." The materials are for library use only. The Maine State Library is in Augusta. The telephone number is 207-287-5600. In general, the collection has city, family, state, and town histories; cemetery, church, court (deeds, probate, wills), immigration, and vital (birth, marriage, death/burial) records. Of special value are the more than 90 "repertoires," which are compilations of church and vital records and family genealogies of Maine and the province of Quebec.

Library and Archives Canada maintains a Web site at: www.collectionscanada.ca that is a joint venture to allow users to search the collections of both facilities. There are links to Canadian Biography Online, hundreds of repositories of church and vital records, and aids to researchers.

On the Net, there is a plethora of genealogy sites. Some are fun to use. Many are a hodge-podge of links and scraps of information with wildly varying degrees of reliability. Look to see what references — if any — are given for the information offered.

Cyndi's List, at www.cyndislist.com, is a favorite among genealogists. In early 2006, it had more than 25,000 links to genealogical resources and 180 categories. The Quebec section had 400 links to repositories, agencies, and organizations. Users of the list are urged to seek out and consult the originals of any material cited in the links. That's good advice.

{ J }

jadis: formerly; au temps jadis: in olden times

jumeau, jumelle: twin

{ K }

la kermesse: a fair or festival, often to benefit a good cause

{ L }

lieu de naissance: place of birth

Loiselle marriage index: A priest of the St. Dominic order, Antoin Loiselle, compiled the "Index to the Many Marriages of Quebec and Adjacent Areas," which was originally published in Quebec in 1965. The index is available for use at research facilities that specialize in French-Canadian genealogy.

{ M }

Maine State Library, Augusta: www.state.me.us/msl; telephone 207-287-5600.

majeur: person who has reached adult age

marraine: godmother

matelot: sailor or seaman

Medical history: Along with the genealogy of blood lines, a parallel chart should be constructed to show the medical history of family members. Knowing about chronic illnesses and diseases that run in a family gives members a chance to ward off or minimize health conditions that could be devastating. Death certificates usually contain the cause of death as well as diseases and chronic conditions that lead to the death. A medical dictionary or reliable medical Web site can explain any unfamiliar medical terms. At print time, the National Library of Medicine and the National Institute of Health offered a consumer information site at www.nim.nih.gov/medlineplus.

Memorabilia: Family history is more than just genealogy. Little souvenirs and treasures collected during a lifetime tell of events that were important to that person. Photos or scans of items should be made and labeled with the five W's (who, what, when, where, why). Seeing and holding objects can trigger memories and associations. These are the stories to write out and include in a living family history.

metis: People of combined European and native American descent, typically of white fathers and native mothers. Coureurs des bois and voyageurs often married into a tribe. Their children were the first metis.

Micmac: A nomadic tribe of native Americans who inhabited the easternmost regions of Acadia. They did not grow corn, but relied on hunting, fishing, and gathering for subsistence.

Military records held at the National Archives, copies of veterans' records for service in World War I or II or subsequent service can be ordered by completing forms requested from the National Personnel Records Center (Military Records), NARA, 9700 Page Boulevard, St. Louis, MO 63132. For military service and pension records that predate World War I, request a form from the General Reference Branch (NNRG-P), National Archives and Records Administration, 7th and Pennsylvania Avenue NW., Washington, DC 20408. As these are government agencies, they require the use of the proper form to request any and all information. A personal letter will not fill the billet. A response can take months, but the results are usually worth the wait.

{ N }

natural child: offspring born out of wedlock

New England Historic Genealogical Society, 101 Newbury St., Boston; Web site: www.nehgs.org; telephone: 617-536-5740. There is a $15 entrance fee to use the resources of this research facility for a day, but it's money well spent if the researcher goes prepared with questions and an idea of where to search for the answers. This can be done by accessing the online guides to NEHGS's vast collection, which includes Atlantic Canada finding aids, cartographic materials, cemetery and genealogy sources, and microfilm.

noter: to record

Names: In French-Canadian heritage, most females were given the name Marie as part of their full name. This was often expressed as the initial M. Marie-Madeleine was very common and would have been written: M-Madeleine. Many males had Joseph as a middle name.

{ O }

ouest: west

{ P }

Parish marriage records: Before the establishment of civil records of marriages in 1970, Canadian marriage records were made by church parishes, both Catholic and Protestant. Some records and copies of records have been transferred to regional branches of National Archives Canada. Jeanne Sauve White has compiled a guide to Catholic parishes in Canada to ease the search for marriage records. Her work, "Guide to Quebec Catholic Parishes and Published Parish Marriage Records" (Clearfield Co., 1993), lists all known Catholic parishes and some Protestant ones; the county in which the parish is located; a cross reference to the archives that holds the records for that county; and notes about any compilation of records for a parish or county.

parrain: godfather

Preponderance of evidence: Names, dates, and other "facts" are considered correct only until they are proven wrong. The closer the recording is to the original source or time, the more reliable it usually is, but even an original can be wrong. Distraught relatives and friends might give misinformation for a death

record. A groom might forget the exact date of the bride's
birthday. No record is guaranteed to be 100 percent accurate.

PRDH (Le programme de recherche en demographie historique /
Research Program in Historical Demography): The PRDH is "a
repertory of vital events (in Quebec) 1621-1799," "a
genealogical dictionary of families, 1621-1765," and "a
repertory of couples and finial relations, 1621-1799." Source:
www.genealogie.umontreal.ca. The program was created to
provide demographic data and is used for studies in history,
medicine, linguistics, anthropology, biology, genetics, and
genealogy. Data was gathered from Quebec province parish
registers of the seventeenth and eighteenth centuries, which were
accepted legal proof of the status of an individual through
baptism, marriage, and burial records. Also used were civil
records of naturalizations and testimonies, the Parchemin
database of notarial acts, hospital sick lists, and even letters
concerning "dealers in contraband salt."
     Use of the PRDH is by subscription, but there is free,
limited public access.

Primary source: an official document, statement, or certificate
that was issued at the time of the event. For example, a death
certificate is considered a primary source for the deceased's date
of death but a secondary source for the deceased's date of birth.

la propriete: estate; also called les biens.

Published genealogies: Be wary of genealogies published during
the late 1800s. It was an era of great pride but little substance,
high praise and heavy prejudice. Their reference notes and
bibliographies might give great leads to original or reliable
documents, but don't take the genealogy itself at face value.
Question everything. Accept little. Assume nothing.

{ Q }

quintal: a metric measurement; a quintal equals 100 kilos.

{ R }

rapport: written report

le recensement: census

renseignement: information

rentier: person of independent means

Research facilities: Collections at research facilities maintained by governments, libraries, and societies are continually updated, with new resources added and old ones revised. Before visiting, check the facility's Web site or call to verify days and hours of operation. Some repositories require reservations to use their collections.

{ S }

sage-femme: midwife

Secondary source: a statement or record that was made later than the event or as a transcription of the original document. For example, a death certificate is considered a secondary source for the deceased's date of birth but a primary source for the date of death.

sepulture: burial

seigniory: feudal system in which one man holds a large estate, rents land for farming, and collects fees. In France, the "seigneur" was a lord with many privileges. In Canada, the "seigneurie" was a conditional land grant, with the seigneur required to recruit and transport French families willing to clear and settle the land. Seigniories could be bought and sold, bequeathed and inherited. Some Canadian seigniors requested letters of nobility, but the honorary titles were abolished in 1669.

Skeletons in the closet: Genealogists should be ready for surprises. No matter how sedate a family might seem, there will be the occasional black sheep, such as the man shot in bed with another man's wife, and the tragedy of death in a bear trap. Record them all. They are the facts in a family's history and deserve to be told.

sous signe: the undersigned

{ T }

taillandier: tool maker

telecopieur: fax machine

temoin: witness

le testament: legal will

testamentaire: of a will

Treaty of Paris of 1763: This treaty ended the European Seven Years' War between England, France, and Spain. Spain ceded all lands east of the Mississippi to England. France relinquished all claims to land in North America, including Acadia, Canada, and Cape Breton Island, with the exception of a few islands off the coast of Newfoundland, for use by the French fishing fleet. French subjects were allowed to leave with all their possessions if they did so within 18 months of the treaty. Those who remained would retain the right to practice the Catholic religion and continue to use some of the traditional civil regulations, allowing French law and order, which had sustained the colony since its inception, to continue. (This was reinforced by the Quebec Act of 1774.)

Treaty of Utrecht: 1713 treaty between France and England granted Nova Scotia to England and left Cape Breton to France.

This treaty was used as the basis for justifying the diaspora of Acadians from the land as they would not swear allegiance to Britain.

{ U }

University of Maine maintains the Maine Folklife Center and the Fogler Library Special Collections in Orono. The research facilities hold numerous genealogies, transcribed interviews, and New Brunswick parish registers. Contact at 207-581-1661. The Web site is www.library.umaine.edu.

University of Maine at Fort Kent is the location of the Acadian Archives that serves the Saint John Valley. Contact at 207-834-7500. The Web site is www.umfk.maine.edu.

usine: mill or factory

{ V }

veille: day before

veuve: widow/widow of

vieille/vieux: old; vieillesse: old age

Vital records: Birth, marriage, and death records are the bones of genealogy and are called vital records. Guides to how and where to obtain vital records are (at the time of publication): www.usnpl.com/menews.html; www.vitalrecordsguide.com/maine/index.html;   FirstGov.gov; www.maine.gov. In Maine, as of 1892, the state requested that all municipalities provide a copy of vital records to the state government. Some towns took until 1923 to do so. Town clerks are often able to help with records that date prior to 1892, but some records have been lost. Alternatives are church records of baptism, marriage, and burial.

{ W }

Writing the family history: While exploring and compiling all
the records and memorabilia of a family, some writers will be
overwhelmed. Remember to gather everything together, then sit
back and look at it. Organize the material logically.

Women in early Canada retained their maiden name after
marriage, but used their husband's name when referred to as
Madame.

{ X }

X: the mark made on a document by someone unable to write his
or her name; some marks were symbols or simple drawings of
objects for which the person was known, such as an ax for a
woodcutter. An official would witness the making of the mark.

{ Y }

y: here or there; when used in the phrase "il y a," can mean "long
ago."

{ Z }

Zut! Alors! The genealogy's almost done (or the compiler's
taking a breather):
— Spread out the collection of worksheets, notes, and books.
— Stand back and see what is there.
— Organize the material by family, subject, location —
whatever grouping method is logical.
— Photocopy any originals that have not been copied, place
them in sheet protectors, and store them in a fireproof box.
— Place worksheets in binders or folders and label.
— Compose your own résumé and a current biography and place
in the front of the collection. Someday, someone might wonder
who collected the family information.
— Continue to listen to family stories, write them out, and add

them to the collection as the opportunity arises.

— Add photos by placing them in archival-quality photo album sheets with pockets (not self-adhesive sheets) and putting the sheets near the person's story or chart. Don't forget to label every photo on the back and date it.

— Do not include personal financial information, social security numbers, etc.

APPENDIX III

Genealogy of First Families, 1608-1635

During the Middle Ages, after several widespread outbreaks of a plague called the Black Death, middle-class citizens had to resort to pedigree charts to prove their inheritance of the estates of relatives who had died. In this way, family wealth was consolidated, giving people more income and more leisure and spawning the Renaissance of Europe.

Genealogy has become a pastime for both the wealthy and the average citizen who wants to know a family's history, even if it doesn't entail a monetary inheritance. Descendants of the founding families of Quebec have the advantage of the genealogical dictionaries compiled by Cyprien Tanguay and Rene Jette. Using sound genealogy methods, standard references, and Internet resources, people today can draw their family lines back to the eighteenth century and link with the family groups listed in the Tanguay and Jette volumes. From there, it's just a matter of finding a myriad of cousins who were spawned from the same gene pool to create an extended family with a common 400-year history.

The following descriptions of genealogy methods, lineage lists, and pedigree charts will help readers start the process of genealogical research. Though Samuel de Champlain and his wife, Helene Boulle, did not have any children, their companions in Quebec had many. Samuel stood as witness to many weddings, and Helene was godmother to several children who were born while she was in Quebec, from 1620 to 1624.

Lineage lists

When tracing the settlers of Quebec, the first generation to immigrate to Canada from France is called the progenitor. A genealogy that begins with the progenitor then lists all known descendants is called a descending genealogy.

The two most widely used forms of listing a descending genealogy are the Register System of the New England Historic

Genealogical Society and the Modified Register System of the National Genealogical Society Quarterly. Both are very precise and detailed methods that require the use of superscripts for numbering the generations and references and careful use of Roman and Arabic numerals, periods, and symbols.

Using a simplified version of the two Register systems, a genealogical list of the first five generations of the Hebert family is given in Appendix IV. The Heberts, who arrived in Quebec in 1617, were the first to settle in Quebec. The children had been born in France. Given that the father and mother, Louis Hebert and Marie Rollet, were the progenitors, their children would comprise Generation II and their grandchildren would be Generation III. Superscripts and special symbols have been omitted as the five generations are clearly indicated and the references are limited and stated beforehand.

Lineage lists for all of the families whose progenitor resided in Quebec during the lifetime of Samuel de Champlain, whose death occurred in 1635 are included in Appendix IV. They were the Companions of Champlain. Using pedigree charts, as described below, American and Canadian families can follow their own lines back and perhaps link with one of the founding families. The lineages have been carried through the first three generations, with the exception of the Hebert family, which has been followed through five generations.

In the introductory notes concerning the origin of the progenitors of a family, the first generation in Quebec, only the province of France is given. Some sources list the name of the then extant parish and town, but many no longer exist or have been renamed. In addition, the ancient provinces of France have been redistricted and renamed as departments. Family genealogists should refer to the named sources for more detailed information.

Pedigree charts

A system called ahnentafel or Sosa-Stradonitz is often used to chart an ascending genealogy, from the compiler to all known ancestors, following the generations from younger to older. The full ahnentafel method lists all members of a family group. A modified method, call the multi-name system, follows only a direct line and does not include siblings.

The modified method is the most commonly used. The compiler writes genealogy data on a pedigree chart, which resembles the branches of a tree or the footprint of a bird, from which the word pedigree is thought to have been derived, "pied" meaning foot.

On a pedigree chart, the compiler is No. 1. His or her father is No. 2. Mother is No. 3. Paternal grandfather is No. 4. Paternal grandmother is No. 5. Maternal grandfather is No. 6. Maternal grandmother is No. 7. And so on. Note that males have even numbers. Females have odd numbers. A father's number is twice that of a child's. A mother's number is twice that of a child's plus 1.

Each generation is contained within the above numbering system. Generation I is No. 1. Generation II contains Nos. 2 and 3. Generation III contains Nos. 4 through 7. Generation IV contains Nos. 8 through 15. Generation V contains Nos. 16 through 31. Generation VI contains Nos. 32 through 63. Generation VII contains Nos. 64 through 127. Generation VII contains Nos. 128 through 255. Generation IX contains Nos. 256 through 511. Generation X contains Nos. 512 through 1023. Generation XI contains Nos. 1024 through 2047. Generation XII contains Nos. 2048 through 4095. Generation XIII contains Nos. 4096 through 8191. Generation XIV contains Nos. 8192 through 16,383. Generation XV contains Nos. 16,384 through 32,767. Note that the first number in a generation indicates how many members are in that generation.

Finding and verifying the names of all ancestors through each generation is the challenge of genealogy. A family averages three generations per century, though families who tend to marry early can have more.

Pedigree charts do not have enough space for full reference citations. This deficiency can be overcome by compiling a numerical reference list that corresponds to the individual's number on the chart. An example of a standard chart and an abridged example of the pedigree numbering system with full reference citations is included in Appendix V.

Genealogists who pursue a French-Canadian family line past the progenitor might find that church records will be of help into the sixteenth century, the 1500s, which is when the keeping of baptism and marriage records became the norm in France. Earlier than that, civil records of legal transactions could contain mention of individuals.

Appendix IV

Companions of Champlain

The pioneer families of Quebec, who lived, worked, shared, and survived. Through three generations.

Sources: *Dictionnaire genealogique des familles canadiennes depuis la fondation de la colonie jusqu'a nos jours* by Cyprien Tanguay, *Dictionnaire genealogique des familles du Quebec: des origines a 1730* by Rene Jette, and *Dictionary of Canadian Biography Online*.

Generations are indicated by capital Roman numerals (I, II, III). Children are listed in order of birth with lower case Roman numerals (i, ii, iii, iv, etc.) The lists could have been made shorter by not including the offspring who died without issue, but the omission would not have presented the full picture of the hardships endured by the family during the early days in Quebec. Many children died soon after birth or in early childhood from sickness or in youth from accidents or attacks. One family, the Fourniers, had seventeen children, but only seven survived to adulthood. In another family, the one with the most offspring — twenty — recorded in this appendix, the LeGardeur family, eleven children died in infancy; and of the nine who lived beyond childhood, only five are recorded to have had children of their own. The mothers of these families went through the birth and death of ten or eleven babies, and this fact of life in early Quebec should not be forgotten. The lost infants, though in this life but briefly, often were remembered by the family through the giving of the same baptismal name to a child born later on, so two children by the same name can be found in the same generation.

Note that women in early Canada retained their maiden name after marriage.

Children usually were baptized soon after birth, but not necessarily so. Baptism dates are approximate birth dates. Burial often took place the day of death, especially during outbreaks of disease, or very soon afterward.

The locations given in records of births, marriages, and burials might indicate the movement of families from Quebec to new areas. Taking note of the movement can be useful in genealogical research.

Unintentional errors occur in secondary sources, and sometimes in primary ones. Readers are urged to refer to the listed sources and any available primary records when compiling a family genealogy.

Understanding the genealogy

More than just a collection of names and dates, a carefully constructed genealogy can be a small but valuable window to the past of a family and a culture. Just as the view from a window is two way, so is the relationship between the old and the new.

The Social Security Administration compiles lists of the most popular baby names and has done so for more than a hundred years. The top ten names for boys in 2005 included five names that coincide with a list of the most popular names given to male children born in Quebec during Champlain's residency, 1608-1635. These time-honored names are, in order of popularity by the SSA, Michael, Matthew (Mathieu), Ethan (Etienne), Daniel, and Joseph. Other popular boys' names in early Quebec included Jean (John), especially Jean-Baptiste, Charles, Louis, Pierre (Peter), and Francois (Francis).

None of the female names on the SSA popularity list for 2005 were used during the seventeenth century in Quebec. The most popular girls' names given to children born during pioneer days of New France were Marie, especially when hyphenated with another name, such as Marie-Madeleine, Anne, Marguerite, Francoise, Genevieve, and Elisabeth, spelled with an "s," not a "z."

A careful study of the origins of the progenitors has helped correct a preconceived notion that the majority of the early settlers came from the province of Normandy in France. Not so. Of the seventeen families who stayed in Canada and had issue and whose origins are known, a majority, seven families, emigrated from the province of Perche. Normandy came in a close second with five families. Other provinces represented were Brittany, with two families; and Ile de France, Maine, and Picardy, each with one. Champlain was from Saintonge, a small province on the west coast of France, near the jumpoff port of LaRochelle. Later emigrations from France to Canada showed a predominance from Normandy and the densely populated Ile de France.

The most likely reason for the early prominence of Perche, a very small province tucked in between the provinces of Maine, Normandy, and Ile de France (Paris), was the motivation of Robert Giffard, apothecary and surgeon, to populate his seigniory at Beauport. From within his province, Giffard contracted Zacharie Cloutier, a master carpenter; Jean Guyon, a master mason; and Henri Pinguet, a merchant. Gaspard Boucher, a carpenter and farmer, and Jean Juchereau also hailed from Perche. Jean Cote is thought to have been from Perche as well.

One family group among the Companions of Champlain was that of the Langlois sisters, Francoise and her sister Marguerite, who traveled to Quebec with their husbands, respectively, Pierre Desportes and Abraham Martin. Another Langlois, Noel, was among the progenitors, but no evidence of a family relationship with the Langlois sisters has yet been found.

Once settled, the families intermarried, as can be expected. The recorded dates of marriages that took place in the Hebert family from 1621 to 1757 show that the majority of weddings took place in October through February, with the exception of December, in which none seemed to have taken place. October and November, the months following harvest, were the most popular months.

Early French-Canadian families are renowned for having many offspring. The Hebert family was studied through five generations, for reasons of its prominence as the first founding family of New France, the relative completeness of the records, and the manageable size of the data collection for the two surviving children who came from France to Canada with their parents. The number of descendants was limited; and, therefore, more easily followed and documented and the data analyzed.

The number of children in a family group in the Hebert genealogy ranged from one to twenty, for an average of nine children per family. During the five generations examined, an average of thirty-three percent, one out of every three, of the children died in infancy or youth. Half of the children, fifty percent, lived to adulthood and married. Approximately seventeen percent lived to adulthood but remained unmarried, joining a religious order, becoming an explorer, or their fate is unknown.

Using the averages stated above, of nine children, six would live to see adulthood, four or five of them would marry, and one or two of them would not. Placed in this perspective, the size of the average family in early Canada was not unlike the size of families found in typical farming communities throughout North America and elsewhere in the not so distant past.

The events of our history play forward to our future. Establishing relationships between the two will guide our way.

The Genealogy of the Companions of Champlain

The Amiot/Amyot Family

Philippe Amiot and his family arrived in Quebec in 1635.

I. Philippe Amiot (birth and parentage unknown) married about 1625 in the province of Picardy, France, Anne Convent, daughter of Guillaume Convent and Antoinette de Longval of Picardy.

The children of Philippe and Anne (Generation II):

II-i.   Jean Amiot, interpreter for the Jesuits at Trois Rivieres (1645), died in 1648 in Quebec.

II-ii. Mathieu Amiot married 22 Nov. 1650 Marie Miville, daughter of Pierre Miville and Charlotte Maugis. He was an interpreter for the Jesuits in Trois Rivieres.

The children of Mathieu and Marie (Generation III):

III-i.   Charles Amiot, born 20 Oct. 1651 in Quebec, married 1677 Rosalie Duquet.

III-ii. Pierre Amiot, born 27 Jan. 1653 in Quebec, married Louise Taudiere.

III-iii.   Anne-Marie Amiot, born 21 March 1654 in
           Quebec, married 1670 Jean Huard.
III-iv.   Marguerite Amiot, born 24 Jan. 1656 in
           Quebec, married 1670 Jean Joly.
III-v.   Jean-Baptiste Amiot, born 25 June 1658 in
           Quebec, married 1682 Genieve Guyon.
III-vi.   Francoise Amiot, born 12 July 1660 in Quebec,
           married 1675 Charles Gingras.
III-vii.   Jean Amiot, born 10 May 1662 in Quebec, died
           before 1681.
III-viii. Catherine-Ursule Amiot, born 21 April 1664 in
           Quebec, married 1683 Jean Duquet.
III-ix.   Daniel-Joseph Amiot, born 4 Oct. 1665 in
           Quebec, married 1709 Marie Kapiouapnokoue
           (native American).
III-x.   Mathieu Amiot, born 23 Aug. 1667 in Quebec,
           died 1684.
III-xi.   Philippe Amiot, born 9 April 1669 in Quebec,
           married 1694 Marie Harnois.
III-xii.   Jeanne Amiot, born 22 Nov. 1670 in Quebec,
           married 1691 Paul Tessier.
III-xiii. Etienne Amiot, born 10 Nov. 1672 in Quebec,
           married 1708 Jeanne Campagna.
III-xiv.   Marie Amiot, born ca. 1674, died 1714 in
           Montreal.
III-xv.   Marie-Francoise Amiot, born 13 June 1676 in
           St. Augustin, baptized in Quebec, married 1699
           Jean-Baptiste Thibault.
III-xvi.   Genevieve Amiot, born 5 Nov. 1678 St. in
           Augustin, died the 13th or 14th.

The Boucher Family

I. Gaspard Boucher, son of Jacques Boucher and Francoise
Paigne of the province of Perche, France, married 1619 Nicole
Lemaire of the province of Maine, France. Gaspard was a
carpenter and a farmer. He arrived in Quebec in 1634.
The children of Gaspard and Nicole (Generation II):
II-i.   Charles Boucher, born 7 April 1620, died the 17th, in

France.

II-ii. Antoinette Boucher, born 6 Aug. 1621 in France and died there.

II-iii. Pierre Boucher married 1648 Madeleine Chretienne (no offspring). Pierre married 1652 Jeanne Crevier (no offspring).

II-iv. Nicolas Boucher, born 9 Sept. 1625 in France, died in Trois Rivieres.

II-v. Charles Boucher, born 4 March 1628 in France and died there.

II-vi. Marie Boucher, born 22 Jan. 1629 in France, married 1645 Etienne Lafond.

The children of Marie and Etienne (Generation III):

III-i. Jean Lafond, baptized 1646 Trois Rivieres, married 1670 Catherine Senecal.

III-ii. Marie Lafond, born 25 Oct. 1648 Trois Rivieres, died before 1666.

III-iii. Genevieve Lafond, baptized 1652 Trois Rivieres, married 1667 Jean Trottier.

III-iv. Pierre Lafond, baptized 1655 Trois Rivieres, maried 1677 Madeleine Rivard.

III-v. Francoise Lafond, baptized 1658 Trois Rivieres, married 1671 Charles LeSieur.

III-vi. Etienne Lafond, baptized 1661 Trois Rivieres, married 1685 Marie-Madeleine Dubois.

III-vii. Jeanne Lafond, born ca. 1662, died before 1667.

III-viii. Augustin Lafond, born 14 May 1664 Trois Rivieres.

II-vii. Marguerite Boucher, born 28 July 1631 in France, married 1645 Toussaint Toupin.

The children of Marguerite and Toussaint (Generation III):

III-i. a son, born and died 1647 Quebec.

III-ii. Jean Toupin, born 10 Dec. 1648 Quebec, married 1669 Marie Gloria.

III-iii. Marie Toupin, born 19 Aug. 1651 Quebec, married 1668 Pierre Mouet.

III-iv.   Antoine Toupin, born 5 Feb. 1655 Quebec,
           married 1679 Louise Cloutier.

III-v.   Marguerite Toupin, born and died 1659
           Quebec.

III-vi.   Francois Toupin, born 10 June 1660 Quebec,
           died before 1682.

II-viii. Madeleine Boucher married 1647 Urbain Beaudry (no
         offspring).

The Bourdon Family

I. Jean Bourdon, from the province of Normandy, France,
married 9 Sept. 1635 in Quebec, Jacqueline Potel. Jean
arrived in Quebec in 1634 to fill the post of engineer. He also
worked as a surveyor and cartographer. His land grant of 50
acres was called St. Jean. He also received several seigniories,
but they were not developed to any great extent. He acted as
governor of Trois Rivieres in 1645, participated in peace
negotiations with the Iroquois, was appointed clerk of the
Community of Habitants, and served as attorney-general to
the colony. Jacqueline, whose parentage and place of birth are
not known, died in September 1654 from a fall while she was
seven months pregnant.

The children of Jean and Jacqueline (Generation II):

II-i.   Jacques Bourdon, born 26 March 1637 in Quebec, died
           before 1666.

II-ii.   Genevieve Bourdon, born 24 Nov. 1638 in Quebec,
           joined a religious order.

II-iii.   Marie Bourdon, born 1640 in Quebec, joined a
           religious order.

II-iv.   Marguerite Bourdon, born 12 Oct. 1642 in Quebec,
           joined a religious order.

II-v.   Anne Bourdon, born 28 Aug. 1644 in Quebec, joined a
           religious order.

II-vi.   Jean-Francois Bourdon, born 2 Feb. 1647 in Quebec,
           married 1687 La Rochelle, Aunis, France, Jeanne
           Jannier. They and their children lived in France.

II-vii.   Jacques Bourdon, born 30 Sept. 1652 in Quebec, was
           killed by the Iroquois in 1688.

There was no Generation III of this family who lived in Canada.

The Cloutier Family

According to the PRDH, the Cloutier family had the highest number of descendants in Canada by 1800, numbering about 10,850.

I. Zacharie Cloutier, born ca. 1590 in the province of Perche, France, son of Denis Cloutier and Renee Briere, married 1616 in France, Sainte/Xainte Dupont. Zacharie was a master carpenter and was contracted by Robert Giffard, seignior of Beauport, in 1634 and went to Canada in 1635. Zacharie's family is thought to have joined him in Canada in 1635 or 1636. Zacharie was granted a fief at Beauport, which he sold in 1670, when the family moved to a land-grant in Chateau-Richer. His signature mark was the symbol of an ax.

The children of Zacharie and Sainte (Generation II):

II-i.   Zacharie Cloutier, born 16 Aug. 1617 in France, married 4 April 1648 in France, Madeleine Emard, daughter of Jean Emard and Marie Bineau. Zacharie was a carpenter and a member of the Community of Habitants.

The children of Zacharie and Madeleine (Generation III):

III-i.   Barbe-Delphine Cloutier, born in Beaupre, baptized 1650 Quebec, married 1663 Charles Belanger.

III-ii.   Rene Cloutier, baptized 1651 Quebec, married 1672 Marie Leblanc.

III-iii. Sainte Cloutier, born 20 Jan. 1653 Quebec, married 1672 Nicolas Goulet.

III-iv.   Genevieve Cloutier, born 22 Jan. 1655 Quebec, married 1674 Joseph Guyon.

III-v.   Marie-Madeleine Cloutier, born 15 May 1657 Quebec, married 1676 Pierre Gravel.

III-vi.   Marie Cloutier, born ca. 1659, married 1684 Jean Gravel.

III-vii.   Charles Cloutier, born 11 Nov. 1662 Chateau
          Richer, married 1685 Anne Thibault.

III-viii. Pierre Cloutier, born 1 April 1666 Chateau
          Richer, married 1687 Charlotte Guyon.

II-ii.   Jean Cloutier, born 13 May 1620 in France, married 21
Jan. 1648 in Quebec, Marie Martin, daughter of
Abraham and Marguerite Langlois. Jean was a
carpenter in Beaupre.

The children of Jean and Marie (Generation III):

III-i.   a girl, born 6 Oct. 1650 and died the next day.

III-ii.   Jean Cloutier, born 20 Feb. 1652 in Quebec,
          married 1679 Louise Belanger.

III-iii. Marie Cloutier, born 16 Feb. 1655 in Quebec,
          married 1671 Jean-Francois Belanger.

III-iv.   Marguerite Cloutier, born 15 Feb. 1656 in
          Quebec, married 1674 Robert Caron.

III-v.   Louise Cloutier, born ca. 1658, married 1679
          Antoine Toupin.

III-vi.   Anne Cloutier, born 30 May 1659 in Quebec,
          married 1681 Pascal Mercier.

III-vii. Sainte Cloutier, born ca. 1661, married 1681
          Charles Fortin.

III-viii. Joseph Cloutier, born 14 Aug. 1663 in
          Chateau-Richer, died in 1671.

III-ix.   Pierre-Paul Cloutier, born 18 Sept. 1665 in
          Chateau-Richer, died the 25th.

III-x.   Pierre Cloutier, born 15 April 1667 in Chateau-
          Richer, married 1696 Jeanne Verreau.

III-xi.   Francoise Cloutier, born 29 Oct. 1669 in
          Chateau-Richer, married 1686 Antoine Doyon.

III-xii. Angelique-Geneive Cloutier, born 18 Jan. 1672
          in Chateau-Richer, died in 1699.

III-xiii. Agnes Cloutier, born 18 Nov. 1673 in Chateau-
          Richer, married 1691 Joseph Fortin.

III-xiv. Marie-Madeleine Cloutier, born 7 May 1676 in
          Chateau-Richer, married 1693 Julien Maufils.

II-iii. Sainte Cloutier, born 1 Nov. 1622 in France and died
the same year.

II-iv. Anne Cloutier, baptized 1626 in France, married 12
July 1637 in Quebec, Robert Drouin, a brickmaker, son
of Robert Drouin and Marie Dubois of the province of
Perche, France. Robert arrived in Canada ca. 1636, the
year of his marriage contract with Anne, which is the
oldest extant marriage contract in Canada.

The children of Anne and Robert (Generation III):

III-i.   Agnes Drouin, born 16 Jan. 1641 in Beauport
and died the same year.

III-ii.   a girl, born and died in 1641.

III-iii. a child, born and died in 1642.

III-iv.   Genevieve Drouin, baptized Oct. 1643 in
Quebec, married 1656 Romain Trepanier.

III-v.   a boy, born and died in 1645.

III-vi.   Jeanne Drouin, born February 1647 in Quebec,
married 1659 Pierre Maheu.

II-v.   Charles Cloutier, born 3 May 1629 in France, married
20 April 1659 Louise Morin, daughter of Noel Morin
and Helene Desportes.

The children of Charles and Louise (Generation III):

III-i.   Elisabeth-Ursule Cloutier, born 29 July 1660
Quebec, married 1676 Nicolas Gamache.

III-ii.   Marie-Madeleine Cloutier, born 23 Sept. 1662
Chateau Richer, married 1681 Paul Tessier.

III-iii. Marie-Anne Cloutier, born 26 Feb. 1664
Chateau Richer, married 1684 Charles Gariepy.

III-iv.   Jeanne Cloutier, born ca. 1668, married 1687
Claude Gravel.

III-v.   Charlotte Cloutier, born 15 Dec. 1670 Chateau
Richer, died 1687 in Quebec.

III-vi.   Louise Cloutier, born 12 Feb. 1673 Chateau
Richer, married 1695 Nicolas Bonhomme.

III-vii. Charles Cloutier, born 15 May 1674 Chateau
Richer, died 1692.

III-viii. Helene Cloutier, born ca. 1677, married 1696
Pierre Gagnon.

III-xi.   Marie Cloutier, born 9 March 1679 Chateau
Richer, married 1699 Joseph Gagnon.

III-x. Jean-Baptiste Cloutier, born 16 May 1681
        Chateau Richer, married 1702 Anne Morisset.
III-xi. Zacharie Cloutier, born 2 Aug. 1683 Chateau
        Richer, married 1708 Jeanne Bacon.
III-xii. Augustin Cloutier, born 13 Jan. 1686 Chateau
        Richer.
III-xiii. Joseph Cloutier married 1720 Elisabeth Morin.
II-vi. Louise Cloutier, born 18 March 1632 in France,
        married 1645 Francois Marguerie.
Louise and Francois did not have any children.

The Cote/Coste Family

I. Jean Cote, possibly of the province of Perche, France, married
17 Nov. 1635 Quebec, Anne Martin, whose parentage and
place of birth is unknown. Jean arrived in Quebec 20 July
1635.
The children of Jean and Anne (Generation II):
II-i.   Louis Cote, born 25 Oct. 1635 Quebec, married 6 Nov.
        1662 Elisabeth Langlois, daughter of Noel Langlois
        and Francoise Garnier.
        The children of Louis and Elisabeth (Generation III):
        III-i. Marie-Madeleine Cote, born 18 Sept. 1663
                Chateau Richer, married 1682 Louis Lemieux.
        III-ii. Louis Cote, born 31 Jan. 1665 Chateau Richer,
                married 1691 Genevieve Bernier.
        III-iii. Jean Cote, born 6 March 1667 Quebec, died
                1687 Chateau Richer.
II-ii. Simone Cote, baptized 1637 Quebec, married 1649
        Pierre Soumande, son of Louis Soumande and
        Guillemette Savoreau of the province of Guyenne,
        France. Pierre was a master toolmaker.
        The children of Simone and Pierre (Generation III):
        III-i. Louis Soumande, born 14 May 1652 Quebec,
                became a priest.
        III-ii. Jean Soumande, born 11 April 1654 Quebec,
                died between 1667 and 1681.
        III-iii. Marie Soumande, born 1 Aug. 1655 Quebec,
                married 1670 Joseph Mignault.

III-iv. Pierre Soumande, born 4 Dec. 1656 Quebec, died 1657.

III-v. Anne Soumande, born 14 Jan. 1658 Quebec, maried 1672 Francois Hazeur.

III-vi. Pierre Soumande, born 14 Sept. 1659 Quebec, was a captain of the merchant marine.

III-vii. Jean Soumande, born 14 Oct. 1661 Quebec, died between 1667 and 1681.

III-viii. Louise Soumande, born 16 May 1664 Quebec, joined a religious order.

III-ix. Jeanne Soumande, born 24 May 1666 Quebec, died 1677.

III-x. Simon Soumande, born 1 Jan. 1668 Quebec, died 1695.

III-xi. Jean Soumande, born 6 Oct. 1669 Quebec, married 1698 Anne Chaspoux.

III-xii. Joseph Soumande, born 15 Nov. 1670 Quebec, died 1687 Montreal.

III-xiii. Marie-Madeleine Soumande, born 13 Jan. 1672 Quebec, joined a religious order.

II-iii. Martin Cote, born 12 July 1639 Quebec, married 25 July 1667 Chateau Richer, Suzanne Page, daughter of Raymond and Madeleine Bergeron.

The children of Martin and Suzanne (Generation III):

III-i. Jean Cote, born 6 Sept. 1668 Chateau Richer, died soon after.

III-ii. Jean Cote, born 18 March 1670 Ste. Famille Ile d'Orleans, married 1694 Marie-Anne Langlois.

III-iii. Marguerite Cote 27 July 1672 Ste. Famille Ile d'Orleans, married 1692 Andre Paren.

III-iv. Marie-Madeleine Cote, born 2 Aug. 1675 Ste. Famille Ile d'Orleans, married 1691 Guillaume Couture.

III-v. Pierre Cote, born and died 1677 St. Pierre Ile d'Orleans.

III-vi. Anne Cote, born 2 April 1679 Ste. Famille Ile d'Orleans, died 1695.

III-vii. Elisabeth Cote, born 17 Nov. 1681 St. Pierre,
married 1703 Pierre Pichet.

III-viii. Pierre-Martin Cote, born 7 March 1684 St.
Pierre, married 1707 Marie Baillargeon.

III-ix. Louis Cote, born 28 June 1686 St. Pierre, died
1712.

II-iv. Mathieu Cote, born 6 July 1642 Quebec, married 11
Sept. 1667 Elisabeth Gravel, daughter of Masse Gravel
and Marguerite Tavernier, probably of Perche, France.
The children of Mathieu and Elisabeth (Generation III):

III-i. Marie-Charlotte Cote, born 6 Oct. 1670 Ste.
Famille Ile d'Orleans, married 1688 Francois
Gosselin.

III-ii. Martin Cote, born 22 Jan. 1673 Ste. Famille Ile
d'Orleans, married 1698 Marguerite Ferland.

III-iii. Marie-Anne Cote, born 6 April 1675 Ste.
Famille Ile d'Orleans, joined a religious order.

III-iv. Louise Cote, born and died 1677 Ile d'Orleans.

III-v. Marie-Genvieve Cote, born 1678, died before
1681.

III-vi. Joseph Cote, born and died 1681.

III-vii. Pierre Cote, born 8 Feb. 1684 St. Pierre Ile
d'Orleans, married 1707 Genevieve Ferland.

III-viii. Mathieu Cote, born 5 March 1686 St. Pierre Ile
d'Orleans, married 1710 Francoise Dupil.

III-ix. Jean-Baptiste Cote, born 16 Sept. 1688, died
1689.

II-v. Jean Cote, born 25 Feb. 1644 Quebec, married 11 Nov.
1669 Anne Couture, daughter of Guillaume and Anne
Emard. Jean was the captain of the militia on Ile
d'Orleans in 1704 and 1707. He married 25 Feb. 1686
Quebec, Genevieve Verdon, daughter of Vincent
Verdon and Genevieve Pelletier.
The children of Jean and Anne (Generation III):

III-i. Jean-Baptiste Cote, born 24 Aug. 1670
Quebec, married 1695 Francoise-Charlotte
Choret.

III-ii. Noel Cote, born 11 Dec. 1672 Quebec, married

        1696 Marie-Madeleine Drouin.

III-iii.   Marguerite Cote, born ca. 1674, joined a
         religious order.

III-iv.   Marie Cote, born ca. 1676, joined a religious
         order.

III-vi.   Pierre Cote, born 22 Nov. 1679 St. Pierre Ile
         d'Orleans, married 1707 Marie-Charlotte
         Rondeau.

III-vi.   Guillaume Cote, 7 Nov. 1681 St. Pierre Ile
         d'Orleans, married 1719 Clotide Amelot.

III-vii.   Anne Cote, born 27 July 1683 St. Pierre, joined
         a religious order.

The children of Jean and Genevieve (Generation III):

III-i.   Marie-Charlotte Cote, born 31 Oct. 1686 St.
         Pierre, married 1705 Francois Tinon.

III-ii.   Joseph Cote, born 28 June 1689 St. Pierre,
         married 1711 Therese Huot.

III-iii.   Marie (called Genevieve) Cote, born 31 Aug.
         1691 St. Pierre, married 1709 Louis Boissel.

III-iv.   Jaques (called Gabriel) Cote, baptised 1693 St.
         Pierre, died 1707.

III-v.   Jean-Marie Cote, born 1 March 1696 St. Pierre,
         married 1716 Madeleine Huot.

III-vi.   Francois Cote, born 7 Feb. 1698 St. Pierre.

III-vii.   Ignace Cote, born 24 March 1700 Baie St.
         Paul.

III-viii.   Gabriel Cote, born 2 Feb. 1702 Baie St. Paul.

III-ix.   Charles Cote, born 5 Sept. 1704 St. Pierre.

III-x.   Thomas Cote, born 28 March 1707 St. Pierre.

III-xi.   Marie Cote, born 6 March 1711 L'Ange-
         Gardien.

II-vi.   Noel Cote, born 4 May 1646 Quebec, married 13 Feb.
      1673 Helene Graton, daughter of Claude and
      Marguerite Moncion.

The children of Noel and Helene (Generation III):

III-i.   Jean-Baptiste Cote, born 16 Nov. 1674 Ste.
         Famille, died before 1681.

III-ii.   Louise Cote, born 25 Oct. 1676 Ste. Famille,
           married 1698 Anet Jaladon.
III-iii.   Genevieve Cote, born 17 June 1679 Ste.
           Famille, died 1706.
III-iv.   Jean-Baptiste Cote, born 16 July 1682 St.
           Pierre, died 1712.
III-v.   Pierre Cote, born and died 1684 St. Pierre.
III-vi.   Jacques Cote, born 5 March 1688 St. Pierre,
           married 1706 Madeleine Rondeau.
III-vii.   Marie-Charlotte Cote, born and died 1688 St.
           Pierre.
III-viii. Anne Cote, born 27 Jan. 1690 St. Pierre,
           married 1710 Francois Pauze.
III-ix.   Joseph Cote, born 22 Oct. 1692 St. Laurent,
           married 1714 Marie-Anne Lambert.
III-x.   Augustin Cote, born 1 Sept. 1695 St. Pierre,
           married 1720 Madeleine Baillargeon.
II-vii. Marie Cote, born 11 Jan. 1648 Quebec, died the 25th.
II-viii. Louise Cote, born 10 April 1650 Quebec, married 4
    Nov. 1663 Jean Grignon, son of Antoine and Suzanne
    Supet. Both Louise and Jean died in La Rochelle,
    France, where their second child, Suzanne, was born in
    1668. The only child of Louise and Jean who was born
    in Quebec was their oldest child, Marie-Madeleine,
    born 3 Aug. 1665. Her burial was on the 10th.

The Couillard/Couillart Family

I. Guillaume Couillard, son of Guillaume Couillard and
   Elisabeth de Vesins of the province of Brittany, France,
   married 26 Aug. 1621 Quebec, Guillemette Hebert, daughter
   of Louis Hebert and Marie Rollet. Guillaume was a seaman,
   caulker, and carpenter. He arrived in Quebec in 1613. After
   his father-in-law's death in 1627, Guillaume farmed the
   Hebert land for the family. He was granted land for cultivation
   by Champlain in 1627, and in 1639 was appointed to the role
   of clerk of cleared lands and food production for Quebec. He
   was the first man to use a plow in Canada, receiving one from
   France and putting it into the ground in 1628. He and his wife

and mother-in-law cared for Champlain's two adopted native girls, named Charity and Esperance, during the 1629-32 occupation of Quebec by the Kirke brothers. Guillemette often filled the role of godmother to native children. Violins were played at the wedding of the Couillard's third daughter, Elisabeth, which was the first known use of the instrument in Quebec. Guillaume died in 1663. Guillemette sold land in 1666 to Bishop Laval for use as a seminary. Guillemette died in 1684 in Quebec, spending her last years as a boarder in a convent.

The family line is included in the Hebert family lineage. The progenitor, Guillaume Couillard, married into the Hebert family, which has been delineated through five generations.

The Delaunay Family

I. Pierre Delaunay, son of Gilles Delaunay and Denise/Louise Dubois of the province of Maine, France, married 7 Nov. 1645 Quebec, Francoise Pinguet, daughter of Henri Pinguet and Louise Lousche (see Pinguet Family). Pierre arrived in Quebec 1635 and was killed by the Iroquois 1654.

The children of Francoise and Pierre (Generation II):

II-i.   Charles Delaunay, born 1648 Quebec, married 12 Dec. 1695 Montreal, Marie-Anne Legras, daughter of Jean Legras and Marie-Genevieve Mallet. Charles worked for the Jesuits at a mission to the Iroquois and was contracted in 1686 to explore the West. He was also a merchant and a tanner.

The children of Charles and Marie-Anne (Generation III):

III-i.   Marie-Josephe Delaunay, born 21 April 1697 Montreal, married 1714 Gabriel Lenoir.

III-ii.   Marie-Marguerite Delaunay, born 28 June 1699 Montreal, married 1724 Pierre Lebeau.

III-iii.   Anne-Louise Delaunay, born 25 July 1701 Montreal, died 1706.

III-iv.   Genevieve-Marguerite Delaunay, born 1703 Montreal.

III-v.   Charles Delaunay, born 31 May 1704
          Montreal, married 1722 Elisabeth Brunet.
III-vi.   Michel-Daniel Delaunay, born 1705 Montreal.
III-vii. Francois Delaunay, born 1707 Montreal.
III-viii. Marie-Elisabeth Delaunay, born 24 March
          1708 Montreal, died 1727.
III-ix.   Francoise-Michelle Delaunay, born 1709
          Montreal.
III-x.   Louis Delaunay, born 1711 Montreal.
III-xi.   Joseph Delaunay, born 1712 Montreal.
III-xii. Jean Delaunay, born 1715 Montreal, died 1728.
III-xiii. Marie-Angelique Delaunay, born 1717
          Montreal.
III-xiv. Marie-Catherine Delaunay, born 1721
          Montreal.
II-i.   Louis Delaunay, born 1650 Quebec, married ca. 1694
        Marie-Catherine Aouacamgo, a native American.
        The children of Louis and Marie-Catherine (Generation
        III):
III-i.   Jean-Jacques Delaunay, born 1695 Kaskaskia.
III-ii.   Charles Delaunay, born 1698 Kaskaskia.
III-iii. ? Marie-Therese Delaunay, born ca. 1696, died
          1714.
II-iii. Henri Delaunay, born 3 Feb. 1653 Quebec, married 6
        Nov. 1679 Beauport, Francoise Crete. Henri was a
        wheelwright.
        The children of Henri and Francoise (Generation III):
III-i.   Marie-Francoise Delaunay, born 29 Oct. 1680
          Quebec, married 1697 Jean Brochu.
III-ii.   Philippe Delaunay, born 1682 Quebec.
III-iii. Marguerite Delaunay, born 26 March 1684
          Quebec, married 1700 Pierre Belanger.
III-iv.   Catherine Delaunay, born 16 Jan. 1686
          Quebec, married 1704 Jean-Baptiste Hubert.
III-v.   Genevieve Delaunay, born 1687 Quebec,
          joined a religious order.
III-vi.   Joseph Delaunay, born 10 April 1689 Quebec.
III-vii. Rene Delaunay, born 15 Feb. 1691 Quebec,

died 1725.

III-viii. Marie-Barbe Delaunay, born 20 Nov. 1692
Quebec, married 1722 Jean-Baptiste
Monmellian.

III-ix. Marie-Madeleine Delaunay, born 1694
Quebec, married 1712 Louis Enouille.

III-x. Marie-Angelique Delaunay, born and died
1695 Quebec.

III-xi. Pierre Delaunay, twin, born 21 Dec. 1696
Quebec, died 1703.

III-xii. Jean Delaunay, twin, born 21 Dec. 1696.

III-xiii. Marie-Angelique Delaunay, born 8 Aug. 1698
Quebec, married 1725 Antoine Parent.

III-xiv. Marie-Anne Delaunay, born 25 Sept. 1700
Quebec.

III-xv. Genevieve Delaunay, born 15 Nov. 1702
Quebec.

The Desportes Family

I. Pierre Desportes, of the province of Normandy, France,
married Francoise Langlois, whose origin is unknown. Pierre
arrived in Quebec ca. 1619 with Abraham Martin, his brother-
in-law. Their wives were sisters. His only official act that still
exists is a petition to the king in 1621 that he signed on behalf
of the inhibitants of Quebec.

The children of Pierre and Francoise (Generation II):

II-i. Helene Desportes, born ca. 1620, one of the first
children of European descent to be born in Canada,
married in 1634 Guillaume Hebert, son of Louis Hebert
and Marie Rollet. Guillaume died in 1639. Madame
Champlain, wife of Samuel, was Helene's godmother.
When Samuel de Champlain died, he bequeathed 300
livres, the average annual wage in 1635, to Helene. As
an adult, Helene was a midwife in Quebec.

The children of Helene and Guillaume (Generation III):

III-i. Joseph Hebert, baptized 1636 Quebec, married
1660 Marie-Charlotte de Poitiers.

III-ii.   Francoise Hebert, born 1638, married 1651,
          Guillaume Fournier.
III-iii. Angelique Hebert, baptized 1639 Quebec, died
          before 1666.
Helene married 9 Jan. 1640 Noel Morin, a wheelwright, son of
Claude Morin and Jeanne Moreau of Brie, France.
          The children of Helene and Noel (Generation III):
III-i.   Agnes Morin, born 21 Jan. 1641 in Quebec,
          married 1653 in Quebec, Nicolas Gaudry;
          married 1671 in Quebec, Ignace Bonhomme.
III-ii.   Germain Morin, born 14 Jan. 1642 Quebec,
          became a priest.
III-iii. Louise Morin, born 27 April 1643 Qubec,
          married 1659 Charles Cloutier.
III-iv.   Nicolas Morin, born 26 April 1644 Quebec.
III-v.   Jean Morin, born 22 May 1645 Quebec,
          married 1667 Catherine DeBelleau, born 1639,
          daughter of Francois and Anne DeBreda of the
          province of Picardy, France. Jean was also
          known as Jean-Baptiste. He was a member of
          the Conseil Souverain and a merchant.
III-vi.   Marguerite Morin, born 29 Sept. 1646 Quebec,
          died 17 Oct. 1646.
III-vii. Helene Morin, born 30 Sept. 1647 Quebec,
          died 9 May 1661.
III-viii. Marie Morin, born 19 March 1649 Quebec,
          joined a religious order.
III-ix.   Alphonse Morin, born 13 Dec. 1650 Quebec,
          married 1670 Marie-Madeleine/Marguerite
          Normand, born 1651, daughter of Jean-Baptiste
          Normand, merchant of Paris, and Catherine
          Rageot of Sens, France; later married
          Angelique Destroismaisons, aka
          DesTroisMaisons ("of three houses").
III-x.   Noel Morin, born 12 Oct. 1652 Quebec, died
          before 1666.
III-xi.   Charles Morin, born 29 Aug. 1654 Quebec,
          died 4 Oct. 1671.

III-xii. Marie-Madeline Morin, born 28 Dec. 1656
Quebec, married 1673 in Quebec, Gilles
Rageot, born 1642, son of Isaac Rageot and
Louise Duret of St. Jean de l'Aigle, Evreux,
France. Gilles was the first royal notary in New
France.

The Giffard Family
The Giffard family arrived in Quebec in 1634.
I. Robert Giffard, born 1587 in the province of Perche, France, a
son of Marc Giffard and Jeanne Poignant, married 12 Feb.
1628 in Perche, Marie Regnouard/Renouard, born 8 Sept.
1599 in Perche, daughter of Charles Renouard and Jacqueline
Michel. Robert was an apothecary and surgeon and said to be
the first doctor of the Hotel-Dieu (hospital) of Quebec. He had
first built a hunting cabin near Beauport ca. 1627, was
captured by the Kirke brothers in 1628, but returned to
Canada in 1634 with his wife and two children. They settled
one of the first seigniories in Canada. Giffard was credited
with bringing several families to Canada as settlers for the
Company of New France. Robert died 14 April 1668 in
Beauport. His son Joseph died without offspring, so his
branch of the family name did not continue in Canada. His
other son returned to France.
The children of Robert and Marie (Generation II):
II-i.   Marie Giffard, called Marie-Francoise, born 4 Dec.
1628, married 21 Nov. 1645 Jean Juchereau, son of
Jean Juchereau and Marie Langlois.
The children of Marie and Jean (Generation III):
III-i.   Noel Juchereau, born 3 July 1647 Quebec,
became a Jesuit brother.
III-ii.   Jeanne-Francoise Juchereau, born 1 May 1650
Quebec, joined a religious order.
III-iii.   Marie-Louise Juchereau, born 9 Sept. 1652
Quebec, married 1668 Charles Aubert.
III-iv.   Charlotte Juchereau, born 22 Aug. 1655
Quebec, joined a religious order.

III-v.   Paul-Augustin Juchereau, born 8 July 1658
         Quebec, did not marry.

III-vi. Marie Juchereau, born 26 April 1660 Quebec,
         joined a religious order.

III-vii. Denis-Joseph Juchereau, born 20 June 1661
         Quebec, an explorer, did not arry.

II-ii. Charles Giffard, born 30 Dec. 1631 France, returned to
        France in 1646.

II-iii. Francoise Giffard, born 12 June 1634 Quebec, joined a
        religious order.

II-iv. Louise Giffard, born 30 March 1639 Quebec, married
        1652 Charles de Lauzon. Their only child, Marie-
        Josephe, was born 14 Oct. 1656 in Quebec. Louise died
        31 October. Charles and his daughter eventually
        returned to France and both died in La Rochelle.

II-v.   Marie Giffard, called Marie-Therese, born Quebec,
        married 22 Sept. 1649 Nicolas Juchereau, son of Jean
        Juchereau and Marie Langlois.
        The children of Marie and Nicolas (Generation III):

III-i.   Marie Juchereau, called Marie-Anne, born 14
         Aug. 1653 Quebec, married 1669 Francois
         Pollet.

III-ii. Charles Juchereau, born 26 Dec. 1655 Quebec,
         married 1692 Denise-Catherine Migeon.

III-iii. Ignace Juchereau, born 5 Aug. 1658 Quebec,
         married 1683 Marie-Catherine Peuvret.

III-iv. Charlotte-Francoise Juchereau, born 3 Feb.
         1660 Quebec, married 1680 Francois Viennay-
         Pachot.

III-v.   Madeleine-Louise Juchereau, born 11 July
         1662 Quebec, married 1694 Joseph-Alexandre
         de l'Estringuant.

III-vi. Therese Juchereau, born 8 Nov. 1664 Quebec,
         married 1684 Pierre de Lalande.

III-vii. Nicolas Juchereau, born 30 Aug. 1666 Quebec,
         died before 1681.

III-viii. Catherine Juchereau, born 18 Oct. 1668
         Quebec, joined a religious order.

III-ix.   Francois Juchereau, born 21 Sept. 1670
Quebec, had a child with Etiennette Normand.

III-x.   Joseph Juchereau, born 8 Jan. 1673 Quebec,
did not marry.

III-xi.   Louis Juchereau, born 17 Sept. 1676 Quebec,
an explorer, did not marry.

III-xii.   Jacqueline-Catherine Juchereau, born 4 Sept.
1679, married 1699 Pierre Aubert.

II-vi.   Joseph Giffard, born 28 Aug. 1645 Quebec, married 22
Oct. 1663 Quebec, Michelle-Therese Nau. They did not
have children.

The Guyon Family

I. Jean Guyon, son of Jacques Guyon and Marie Huet of the
province of Perche, France, married 2 June 1615 in France,
Mathurine Robin, possibly daughter of Eustache Robin and
Madeleine Avrard. Jean and Mathurine brought several of
their children with them to settle in Beauport in 1634 with the
Cloutier and Giffard families. Jean was a master mason and
was contracted by Robert Giffard to work in Canada.

The children of Jean and Mathurine (Generation II):

II-i.   Barbe Guyon, born 19 April 1617 in France, married
11 Feb. 1632 Pierre Paradis.

The children of Barbe and Pierre (Generation III):

III-i.   Charlotte Paradis, born 4 April 1634 in France,
died 1700 in France.

III-ii.   Marguerite Paradis, born and died in France.

III-iii.   Marie Paradis, married 1656 Guillaume
Baucher.

III-iv.   Jacques Paradis, born in France, married 1668
Jeanne-Francoise Milloir.

III-v.   Guillaume Paradis, born in France, married
1670 Genevieve Milloir.

III-vi.   Pierre Paradis, born in France, married 1674
Jeanne Milloir.

III-vii.   Jean Paradis, born in France, married 1679
Jeanne Paquet.

III-viii. Madeleine Paradis, born 1653 Quebec, married
          1667 Nicolas Roussin.
III-ix. Marie-Madeleine Paradis, born 12 Jan. 1656
          Quebec, married 1674 Robert.
III-x.   Jean Paradis, born 1 July 1658 Quebec,
          married 1693 Chatherine Batailler.
III-xi. Louise Paradis, born 5 Aug. 1661 Quebec,
          married 1678 Thomas Mezeray.
II-ii. Jean Guyon, born 1 Aug. 1619 in France, married 27
      Nov. 1645 Elisabeth Couillard, daughter of Guillaume
      Couillard and Guilemette Hebert.
The children of Jean and Elisabeth (Generation III): See III-iv.
under Hebert Family.
II-iii. Simon Guyon, born 2 Sept. 1621 in France, married 10
      Nov. 1653 Louise Racine, daughter of Etienne Racine
      and Marguerite Martin. Simon was a carpenter.
      The children of Simon and Louise (Generation III):
      III-i.   Jean Guyon, born 3 Oct. 1659 Quebec, became
             a priest.
      III-ii. Marie Guyon, born 25 March 1662 Chateau
             Richer, Guyon 1681 Guillaume Thibault.
      III-iii. Marguerite Guyon, born 7 Sept. 1665 Chateau
             Richer, married 1686 Louis Damours.
      III-iv. Louise Guyon, born 30 April 1668 Chateau
             Richer, maried 1684 Charles Thibault.
      III-v.   Charlotte Guyon, born 2 April 1671 Chateau
             Richer, married 1687 Pierre Cloutier.
      III-vi. Marie-Angelique Guyon, born 17 July 1673
             Chateau Richer, married 1692 Richard Maret.
      III-vii. Barbe Guyon, born ca. 1675.
II-iv. Marie Guyon, born 18 March 1624 in France, married
      12 July 1637 in Quebec Francois Belanger, probably of
      Normandy, France. Francois was a mason and captain
      of the military at Beaupre from 1663 to 1677.
      The children of Marie and Francois (Generation III):
      III-i.   Charles Belanger, born 1640 Quebec, married
             1663 Barbe-Delphine Cloutier.
      III-ii. Marie-Madeleine Charles Belanger, born 1643

Quebec, married 1656 Bertrand Chenay.

III-iii. Marguerite Belanger, born 1645 Quebec, married 1663 Antoine Berson.

III-iv. Jean-Francois Belanger, born 1648 Quebec, married 1671 Marie Cloutier.

III-v. Charlotte-Francoise Belanger, born 25 June 1650 Quebec, married 1665 Jean Langlois.

III-vi. Mathurine Belanger, born 1652 Quebec, married 1673 Jean Maheu.

III-vii. Louis Belanger, born 1654 Quebec, married 1682 Marguerite Lefrancois.

III-viii. Louise Belanger, born ca. 1657, married 1679 Jean Cloutier.

III-ix. Genevieve Belanger, born ca. 1659, married 1682 Guillaume Ferte.

III-x. Guillaume Belanger, born and died 1661 Chateau Richer.

III-xi. Jacques Belanger, born 1662 Chateau Richer, married 1691 Elisabeth Thibault.

III-xii. Anne Belanger, born 1664 Chateau Richer, died 1665.

II-v. Marie Guyon, born 29 Jan. 1627 in France.

II-vi. Claude Guyon, born 22 April 1629 in France, married 7 Feb. 1655 Quebec, Catherine Colin, daughter of Jacques Colin and Madeleine de Baubise of Paris, France.

The children of Claude and Catherine (Generation III):

III-i. Jean Guyon, born 10 July 1656 Quebec, married 1688 Marie Pepin.

III-ii. Marie-Madeleine Guyon, born 1657 Quebec, married 1671 Gervais Rocheron.

III-iii. Louise Guyon, born 15 Jan. 1660 Quebec, married 1682 Pierre Racine.

III-iv. Marguerite Guyon, born 12 Feb. 1662 Chateau Richer, died 1663.

III-v. Claude Guyon, born 4 Oct. 1663 Ile d'Orleans, married 1688 Marie-Madeleine Lehoux.

III-vi.   Catherine Guyon, born 10 Dec. 1664 Chateau Richer, married 1683 Etienne.

III-vii.   Marie-Anne Guyon, born 18 May 1666 Chateau Richer, joined a religious order.

III-viii. Jacques Guyon, born 5 Sept. 1667 Quebec, died 1688.

III-ix.   Elisabeth Guyon, born 21 Aug. 1669 Quebec, joined a religious order.

III-x.   Renee Guyon, born 1670 Ile d'Orleans, married 1688 Jean Pepin.

III-xi.   Francoise Guyon, born 21 Sept. 1672 Ile d'Orleans, married 1689 Charles Gravel.

III-xii.   Gervais Guyon, born 18 May 1676 Ile d'Orleans, married 1695 Catherine Lehoux.

II-vii. Denis Guyon, born 30 June 1631 in France, married 21 Oct. 1659 Elisabeth Boucher, daughter of Francois Boucher and Florence Gareman. Denis was a merchant in Quebec in the lower village.

The children of Denis and Elisabeth (Generation III):

III-i.   Bertrand Guyon, born 7 May 1662 Quebec, died the 29th.

III-ii.   Jacques Guyon, born 1 Nov. 1663 Quebec, married 1688 Louise Niel.

III-iii. Francois Guyon, born 3 March 1666 Quebec, married 1689 Marie-Anne Roberge.

III-iv. Denis Guyon, born 1669 Quebec, died before 1681.

III-v.   Marie-Therese Guyon, born 6 April 1671 Quebec, married 1687 Antoine de Lamothe.

III-vi.   Joseph Guyon, born 16 Jan 1674 Quebec, died before 1681.

III-vii.   Elisabeth Guyon, baptized 1679 Sorel, died 1681 Quebec.

III-viii. Charles-Louis Guyon, born 17 Nov. 1681 Quebec, died 1682.

III-ix.   Jeanne-Catherine Guyon, born 28 July 1683 Quebec, died 1684.

II-viii. Michel Guyon, called Rouvray/duRouvray, born 3

March 1634 in France, married 4 Sept. 1662 Quebec,
Genevieve Marsolet, daughter of Nicolas Marsolet and
Marie Barbier. Michel was a ship carpenter.
The children of Michel and Genevieve (Generation III):

III-i.   Joseph Guyon, born 1664 Quebec, died before
1681.

III-ii.   Genevieve Guyon, born 16 Jan. 1666 Quebec,
married 1682 Jean-Baptiste Amiot.

III-iii.   Louis Guyon, born and died 1667 Chateau
Richer.

III-iv.   Michel Guyon, born 1669 L'ange-Gardien.

III-v.   Marie-Elisabeth Guyon, born 16 July 1671
Quebec, married 1691 Jean-Baptiste Lemoine.

III-vi.   Jean-Baptiste Guyon, born 1673 Quebec, died
1700 La Rochelle.

III-vii.   Anne Guyon, born 16 May 1675 Quebec,
married 1695 Laurent Renaud.

III-viii.   Charles Guyon, born 17 Feb. 1677 Quebec,
died before 1681.

III-ix.   Suzanne (called Marguerite) Guyon, born 20
Feb. 1679 Quebec, married 1696 Pierre
Constantin.

III-x.   Louis Guyon, born and died 1681 Quebec.

III-xi.   Agelique Guyon, born 25 Aug. 1683 Quebec,
married 1700 Gilles Chauvin.

III-xii.   Mathieu Guyon, born 24 Nov. 1685 Quebec, a
twin.

III-xiii.   Jean Guyon, a twin, born 24 Nov. 1685
Quebec, married 1719 Marie-Louise Couteron.

II-ix. Noel Guyon, born 27 Aug. 1638, died in September.

II-x. Francois Guyon, called Despres, born 7 Dec. 1639
Quebec, married 4 Sept. 1662 Quebec, Marie-
Madeleine Marsolet, daughter of Nicolas Marsolet and
Marie Barbier.
The children of Francois and Marie-Madeleine
(Generation III):

III-i.   Marie Guyon, born 7 April 1664 Quebec,
married 1685 Jean Gauthier.

III-ii.   Joseph Guyon, born 1666 Beauport, married
            1697 Marie-Madeleine Petit.
III-iii.   Anne Guyon, born 26 Dec. 1667 Quebec,
            married 1690 Antoine Legendre.
III-iv.   Marie Guyon, born ca. 1669.
III-v.   Francois Guyon, born 4 Feb. 1671 Quebec.
III-vi.   Marie-Madeleine Guyon, born 4 May 1673
            Beauport, died before 1681.
III-vii.   Nicolas Guyon, born 1675 Beauport, died
            before 1681.
III-viii.   Marie-Suzanne Guyon, born 28 Feb. 1676
            Quebec, died 1703.
III-ix.   Genevieve Guyon, born 28 May 1679 Quebec,
            married 1699 Francois de Chavigny.
III-x.   Marguerite-Francoise Guyon, born 1681
            Beauport.
III-xi.   Angelique Guyon, born 17 Oct. 1684 Beauport,
            married 1712 Francois Margane.
III-xii.   Alexis-Jean Guyon, born 28 April 1687
            Beauport, married 1719 Marie-Simone
            Couillard.

The Hebert Family
The first colonists of Canada
Through five generations

The first family to be established in Quebec, the Heberts arrived
in 1617 from Paris. Their house in Quebec was said to be the
first building constructed in the upper village. At present day, its
location would be between Rue Ste. Famille and Rue Couillard.

I. Louis Hebert, born ca. 1575, son of Nicolas Hebert and
Jacqueline Pajot of Paris, married 1602 in Paris, Marie Rollet.
Louis was an apothecary and played a major role in the
settlement of Quebec. He performed many functions, among
them were doctor, farmer, and post procurer. He died 25 Jan
1627 from a fall while attempting to repair the roof of his
house. Marie opened her home to the small Quebec
community for gatherings and for educating orphaned native
children. She died 27 May 1649 in Quebec.

II-i.   Guillaume Hebert married 1 Oct. 1634 in Quebec,
Helene Desportes, born 1620, daughter of Pierre
Desportes and Francoise Langlois. Helene was one of
the first children of European descent to be born in
Canada. She was a midwife in Quebec. Guillaume died
in 1639.

The children of Guillaume and Helene (Generation III):

III-i.   Joseph Hebert, born 3 Nov. 1636 Quebec,
married 12 Oct. 1660 Marie-Charlotte de
Poitiers, daughter of Pierre-Charles de Poitiers
and Helene de Belleau of the province of
Picardy, France. Joseph died as a prisoner of
the Iroquois.

The child of Joseph and Marie-Charlotte
(Generation IV):

IV-i.   Joseph Hebert born 15 Oct. 1661
Quebec, who died as a youth before
1666, was the last direct male
descendant of Louis Hebert.

III-ii.   Francoise Hebert, born 23 Jan. 1638, married
20 Nov. 1651 Guillaume Fournier, born 1619,
son of Gilles Fournier and Noelle Gagnon of
the province Normandy, France. Francoise was
a midwife and was elected to the Women's
Assembly of the parish.

The children of Francoise and Guillaume
(Generation IV):

IV-i.   Gilles Fournier, born 26 Nov. 1653
Quebec, died in December.

IV-ii.   Marie Fournier, born 5 May 1655
Quebec, married 17 Feb. 1670 in
Quebec, Pierre Blanchet, son of Noel
Blanchet and Madeleine Valet of the
province of Picardy, France.

The children of Marie and Pierre
(Generation V):

V-i.   Pierre-Alphonse Blanchet,
          born 6 July 1672 Quebec,
          married 1699 Louise Gagne.
V-ii.   Guillaume Blanchet, born 15
          June 1674, married 1705
          Marie-Anne Gagne.
V-iii.   Marie-Madeleine Blanchet,
          born 1676, married 1699
          Vincent Chretien.
V-iv.   Jacques Blanchet, born 24
          Aug. 1677, died 1681.
V-v.   Angelique Blanchet, born
          1679, died 1681.
V-vi.   Joseph Blanchet, born and
          died 1681.
V-vii.   Joseph Blanchet, born 1682
          Montmagny.
V-viii.   Jean Blanchet, born 1684
          Montmagny.
V-ix.   Jean Blanchet, born 1685,
          married 1712 Genevieve
          Gagne.
V-x.   Joseph Blanchet, born 1690,
          died 1693.
V-xi.   Louis Blanchet, born 1692,
          died 1693.
V-xii.   Francoise Blanchet, born
          1694 Montmagny, married
          1717 Sebastien Morin.
V-xiii.   Marie-Genevieve Blanchet,
          born 1696 Montmagny.
V-xiv.   Louis Blanchet, born 20 Dec.
          1696, died the 30th.
V-xv.   Louis, born 10 April 1701
          Montmagny, married 1723
          Marie Joly.
IV-iii.   Agathe Fournier, born 10 April 1657
          Quebec, married 1671 Quebec, Louis

Gesseron, called Brulot, son of Louis
Gesseron and Marie Guitard of
LaRochelle, France.
The Children of Agathe and Louis
(Generation V):

V-i.   Joseph Gesseron married
1718 Marie Anne Pelisson.

V-ii.   Marie Gesseron married 1699
Charles Carier.

V-iii. Louise Gesseron married
1707 Pierre Boissel.

V-iv. Charles Gesseron married
1712 Marguerite Nadeau.

IV-iv. Jacquette Fournier, born 10 April 1659
Quebec, married 5 June 1673 Quebec,
Jean Prou, son of Jean Prou and Louise
Vallee of the province of Anjou,
France.
The children of Jacquette and Jean
(Generation V):

V-i.   Denis Prou, born 24 April
1676 Riviere-du-Sud,
married 1699 Marie-Anne
Gagne.

V-ii.   Jean-Baptiste Prou, born 16
Oct. 1677 Riviere-du-Sud,
married 1701 Louise
Rousseau.

V-iii. Louise Prou, born 29 Aug.
1679 Montmagny, married
1700 Pierre Gagne.

V-iv. Pierre Prou, born 8 June 1681
Montmagny, married 1711
Agathe Destroismaisons.

V-v.   Marie-Anne Prou, born 1
Sept. 1683 Montmagny,
married 1703 Jacques
Thibault.

V-vi.   Marie-Barbe Prou, born 25
            March 1685 Montmagny,
            married 1704 Louis Isabel.
V-vii.   Thomas Prou, born 8 Sept.
            1686 Montmagny, married
            1714 Marie-Catherine Caron.
V-viii.   Angelique Prou, born 1688
            Montmagny, married 1705
            Jean-Francois Thibault.
V-ix.   Joseph Prou, born 18 Sept.
            1690 Montmagny, died 1693.
V-x.   Catherine Prou, born 12 July
            1692 Montmagny, died the
            13th.
V-xi.   Anne Prou, born 17 Sept.
            1693 Montmagny, married
            1720 Henri Ruel.
V-xii.   Louis Prou, born 3 April
            1696 Montmagny, married
            1730 Marie Dufresne.
V-xiii.   Joseph Prou, born 27 April
            1698 Montmagny, married
            1729 Dorothee Bouchard.
V-xiv.   Francoise Prou, born 8 Dec.
            1701, married 1729
            Alexandre Gagne.

IV-v.   Joseph Fournier, born 12 July 1661
        Quebec, married 1684 Barbe Girard.
        Six of the couple's seventeen died the
        same day they were born. Four died
        within days of their birth. The
        surviving children of Joseph and Barbe
        (Generation V):

V-i.   Joseph Fournier, born 4 July
            1650 Montmagny, married
            1710 Elizabeth Gagne.
V-viii.   Marie-Barbe Fournier, born
            26 April 1694 Montmagny,

		married 1720 Pierre Lamarre.
	V-xi.	Dorothee Fournier, born 1 Dec. 1697 Montmagny, married 1721 Claude Guimond.
	V-xii.	Jean Fournier, born ca. 1698, married 1717 Louise Joncas.
	V-xiii.	Anne Fournier, born 1 March 1700 Montmagny, married 1729 Jean-Baptiste Gagne.
	V-xv.	Francois Fournier (twin), born 18 April 1704 Montmagny, married 1727 Elisabeth Belanger.
	V-xvi.	Francoise Fournier, born 1704, married Claude Guimont; married 1738 in Cap St. Ignace, Phillippe-Ignace Gravel.
IV-vi.		Marie-Madeleine Fournier, born 17 July 1663 Quebec, died 1664.
IV-vii.		Jean Fournier, born 18 March 1665 Quebec, married 1687 Marie LeRoy/Roy.

The children of Jean and Marie (Generation V):

	V-i.	Nicolas Fournier, born 1690, married 1714 Barbe Tibault.
	V-ii.	Jean Fournier, born 1692, married 1718 Marie-Francoise Dumas.
	V-iii.	Ambroise Fournier, born 1696, married 1729 Genevieve Guillet; married 1734 Genevieve Gamache.
	V-iv.	Cecile Fournier, born 1698, married 1716 Louis Tibault.

V-v.   Anne Fournier, born 1700,
           married 1726 Jean Baptiste
           Durand.
V-vi.   Augustin Fournier, born
           1704, married 1727 Elizabeth
           Gravel; married 1735 Marie-
           Francoise Belanger.
V-vii.   Charles Fournier, born 1708,
           maried 1734 Louise Gravelle.
IV-viii. Simon Fournier, born 27 April 1667 in
         Quebec, married 12 Nov. 1691
         Catherine Rousseau, daughter of
         Thomas Rousseau and Madeleine
         Olivier.
         The children of Simon and Catherine
         (Generation V):
         V-i.   Catherine Fournier, born 8
                   Aug. 1692 Montmangny,
                   married 1709 Pierre
                   Bouchard.
         V-ii.   Marie-Madeleine Fournier,
                   born 10 Feb. 1694
                   Montmagny, married 1715
                   Etienne Fontaine.
         V-iii.   Jean Fournier, baptized 1696
                   Montmagny, married 1720
                   Marie Talbot.
         V-iv.   Genevieve Fournier, baptized
                   1698 Montmagny, married
                   1715 Pierre Gagne.
         V-v.   Marie-Marthe Fournier, born
                   19 Dec. 1699 Montmagny,
                   married 1619 Jean Ruel.
         V-vi.   Simon Fournier, born 7 Feb.
                   1702 Montmagny, married
                   1730 Marthe Bouchard.
         V-vii.   Angelique Fournier, born 25
                   May 1704 Montmagny,

married 1722 Jean
Rollandeau.

V-viii. Marie-Anne Fournier, born
30 March 1707 Montmagny,
married 1726 Francois
Bouffard.

V-ix. a daughter, born and died
1709.

V-x. Joseph Fournier, born 1710
Montmagny.

V-xi. Rosalie, born 19 Jan. 1712
Montmagny, married 1730
Augustin Ruel.

IV-ix. Pierre Fournier, born 24 April 1669
Quebec, married 1695 in St. Thomas,
Marie Isabel. (no married children)

IV-x. Francoise Fournier, born 30 April 1671
Quebec, married 21 April 1686
Montmagny, Jacques Boulay/Boule,
son of Roert Boulay and Francoise
Grenier.

The children of Francoise and Jacques,
all of whom were born in Montmagny
(Generation V):

V-i. Marie Boulay married 1707
Pierre Morin.

V-ii. Jacques Boulay, born 7
March 1689, married 1715
Agathe Morin.

V-iii. Pierre Boulay, born 22 March
1691, married 1716 Marie-
Louise Langlois.

V-iv. Marie-Madeleine Boulay,
born 7 April 1693, married
1718 Denis Morin.

V-v. Joseph Boulay married 1723
Monique Meunier.

V-vi.   Augustin Boulay, baptized 1697, married 1723 Veronique Miville.

V-vii.   Jean-Baptiste Boulay, born 9 May 1699, married 1727 Marie Asselin.

V-viii.   Jacques Boulay, baptized 1700.

V-ix.   Guillaume Boulay, born 11 Sept. 1702, married 1727 Madeleine Miville.

V-x.   Louis Boulay, born 30 Sept. 1704, married 1730 Elisabeth Chasson.

V-xi.   Francois Boulay, born 23 March 1707, married 1730 Genevieve Miville.

V-xii.   Paul Boulay, born 2 Dec. 1708.

V-xiii.   Charles Boulay, born 2 April 1711.

V-xiv.   Martin, born 14 April 1713.

IV-xi.   Louis Fournier, born ca. 1672, married 19 Nov. 1696 Cap-St.-Ignace, Marie Caron, daughter of Pierre Caron and Marie Bernier.

The children of Louis and Marie, all of whom, except Marie-Aimee, were born in Montmagny (Generation V):

V-i.   Louis Fournier, born 30 May 1698, married 1722 Angelique Bosse.

V-ii.   Marie-Genevieve, born 26 Jan. 1700, died 1714.

V-iii.   Marie-Marthe Fournier, born 15 April 1702, married 1719 Pierre Joncas.

V-iv.   Louise Fournier, born 13 Feb.

1705, married 1725 Jacques
Joncas.

V-v.   Jean-Baptiste Fournier, born
23 May 1707, died 1709.

V-vi.   Jean-Baptiste Fournier, born
3 May 1709, died 1713.

V-vii.   Elisabeth Fournier, born 22
July 1711.

V-viii. Francois Fournier, born and
died 1714.

V-ix.   Marie Fournier, born ca.
1716.

V-x.   Marie-Aimee Fournier, born
St.-Pierre-de-la-Riviere-du-
Sud, April 1718.

V-xi.   Marguerite Fournier, born 19
March 1720.

IV-xii. Louis Fournier, born 20 April 1673
Quebec, died in 1674.

IV-xiii. Madeleine Fournier, born 3 Aug. 1675,
married 2 May 1707 in St. Francois de
Sales de l'Ile-Jesus (Laval), Pierre
Laporte, called Saint-Georges, son of
Jean Laporte and Jeanne Minet.
The children of Madeleine and Pierre,
all of whom, except Helene, were born
on l'Ile-Jesus (Generation V):

V-i.   Joseph-Cecile Laporte, born
22 Nov. 1707

V-ii.   Marie-Madeleine Laporte,
born 12 Jan. 1709, married
1725 Louis Devault.

V-iii.   Pierre Laporte, born 12 Dec.
1712.

V-iv.   Helene Laporte, born 26
Sept. 1714 Riviere des
Prairies.

V-v.   Marie Laporte, born 29 July
1716.

IV-xiv. Charles Fournier, born 20 June 1677
Quebec, married 1699 in St. Ignace,
Elizabeth Bouchard. (no married
children)

IV-xv. a daughter, born and died in 1679.

III-iii. Angelique Hebert, born 2 Aug. 1639 Quebec,
died before 1666.

II-ii. Guillemette Hebert, born ca. 1608, married 26 August
1621 Quebec, Guillaume Couillard, son of Guillaume
Couillard and Elisabeth de Vessin of St. Malo,
Brittany, France, or of St-Landry, Paris, France.
Guillaume arrived in Quebec in 1613 as a carpenter and
seaman for the Company of Merchants. Guillemette
inherited a share of the seigniories of her father.
The children of Guillemette and Guillaume (Generation
III):

III-i. Louise Couillard, baptized 30 Jan. 1625
Quebec, married 1637 Olivier Tardif, son of
Jean Tardif and Clemence Houart, of the
province of Brittany, France.
The child of Louise and Olivier (Generation IV):
IV-i.   Pierre Tardif, baptized 1641 Quebec,
died between 1648 and 1666.

III-ii. Marguerite Couillard married 7 Oct. 1637 Jean
Nicolet, son of Thomas Nicolet and Marguerite
de Lamer, of the province of Normandy,
France.
The children of Marguerite and Jean
(Generation IV):
IV-i.   Ignace Nicolet, born ca. 1640 Trois
Rivieres, died the same year.
IV-ii.   Marguerite Nicolet, baptized 1 April
1642 Trois Rivieres, married 9 July
1656 Quebec, Jean-Baptiste
LeGardeur, son of Pierre LeGardeur
and Marie Favery.

V-i.   Pierre LeGardeur, born 10
          March 1657 Quebec, married
          1685 Agathe Saint-Pere.
V-ii.   Guillaume LeGardeur, born 3
          June 1658 Quebec, died the
          4th.
V-iii.   Marie-Anne LeGardeur, born
          13 June 1659 Quebec, died in
          July.
V-iv.   Jean-Paul LeGardeur, born 3
          Oct. 1661 Quebec, married
          1692 Marie-Joseph LeNeuf.
V-v.   Augustin LeGardeur,
          baptized 16 Dec. 1663
          Quebec, married 1697 Marie-
          Charlotte Charet.
V-vi.   Charles LeGardeur, born 28
          Nov. 1664 Quebec, died in
          December.
V-vii.   Alexandre LeGardeur, born
          15 Jan. 1666 Quebec; a
          lieutenant, was killed by the
          Iroquois in 1692 at Montreal.
V-viii.   Charles LeGardeur, born 9
          Feb. 1667 Quebec, died in
          March.
V-ix.   Jean-Baptiste LeGardeur,
          born 26 Feb. 1668 Quebec,
          had a natural child with
          Madeleine-Therese, a native
          American; and a child with
          Marie-Marthe Richaume.
V-x.   Michel LeGardeur, born 16
          June 1671 Repentigny.
V-xi.   Charles-Joseph LeGardeur,
          born 15 Sept. 1676,
          Boucherville.

V-xii.   Louis LeGardeur, born 3
           Nov. 1673 Boucherville.
V-xiii.   Francois LeGardeur, baptized
           1675 Pointe-aux-Trembles,
           was contracted to explore the
           Mississippi.
V-xiv.   Marie-Marguerite LeGardeur,
           born and died in 1675.
V-xv.   Charles LeGardeur, born 26
           March 1677 Repentigny,
           married 1709 Marie-Anne-
           Genevieve Robineau.
V-xvi.   Joseph (called Rene)
           LeGardeur, baptized 1679
           Boucherville, died before
           1681.
V-xvii.   Simon LeGardeur, born 15
           Nov. 1680 Repentigny, died
           1683.
V-xviii.   Noel LeGardeur, born 11
           Feb. 1682 Repentigny.
V-xix.   Marie-Anne LeGardeur, born
           16 April 1683 Repentigny,
           died 1684.
V-xx.   Joseph-Narcisse LeGardeur,
           born 11 June 1684
           Repentigny, died 1703.

III-iii. Louis Couillard, baptized 1629 Quebec,
          married 29 April 1653 Quebec, Genevieve
          Despres, daughter of Nicolas Despres and
          Madeleine Leblanc of Paris. Louis was a
          businessman in Quebec.
          The children of Louis and Genevieve
          (Generation IV):
          IV-i.   Jeanne Couillard, born 3 June 1654
                    Quebec, married 1668 Paul Dupuis.
                    The children of Jeanne and Paul
                    (Generation V):

V-i.	Daniel Dupuis, born 10 Dec. 1669 Quebec, died the 26th.
V-ii.	Anne Dupuis, born 3 July 1671 Quebec, died 1687.
V-iii.	Louis Dupuis, born 3 April 1673 Ile-aux-Oies, died 1688.
V-iv.	Genevieve Dupuis, born 25 April 1675 Ile-aux-Oies, joined a religious order.
V-v.	Simon Dupuis, born 31 March 1677 Ile-aux-Oies, died 1716 Montreal.
V-vi.	Marie Dupuis, born 22 Jan. 1679 Il-aux-Oies, joined a religious order.
V-vii.	Jeanne Dupuis, born 23 April 1681 Il-aux-Oies, died 1702 Quebec.
V-viii.	Marguerite Dupuis, born and died 1683.
V-ix.	Suzanne Dupuis, born 12 May 1684 Ile-aux-Oies, married 1701 Jean Petit.
V-x.	Francoise Dupuis, born 27 Aug. 1686 Ile-aux-Oies, died 1699 Quebec.
V-xi.	Jean-Paul Dupuis, born 29 Jan. 1689 Quebec, died ca. 1717.
V-xii.	Marie-Madeleine Dupuis, born 1690 Quebec, died 1703.
V-xiii.	Jeanne Dupuis, born ca. 1691, died 1703 Quebec.
V-xiv.	Louise-Madeleine, born 14 May 1693 Quebec, joined a religious order.

IV-ii.   Charles Couillard, born 6 Dec. 1655 Quebec, died 1656.

IV-iii.   Jean-Baptiste Couillard, born 2 May 1657 Quebec, married 23 Oct. 1680 Genevieve de Chavigny. They did not have children.

IV-iv.   Louis Couillard, born 28 Nov. 1658 Quebec, married 4 May 1688 Marie Fortin, daughter of Francois Fortin and Marie Jolliet. Louis married Marguerite Belanger 7 Nov. 1712, but she died in 1715 and they did not have children. Louis married Marguerite Fortin 21 June 1716, but she died the next year within days after childbirth, as did the child. Louis married Louise Nolin 31 Jan 1719 Montmagny. They had three children, all born in Montmagny.

The children of Louis and Marie (Generation V):

V-i.   Genevieve Couillard, born 18 July 1689 Quebec, died 1709.

V-ii.   Elisabeth Couillard, born 31 March 1691 Montmagny, married 1716 Louis Cote.

V-iii.   Louise Couillard, born 16 Nov. 1692 Montmagny, died 1693.

V-iv.   Louis Couillard, born 4 Feb. 1694 Montmagny, married 1721 Marthe Cote.

V-v.   Claire-Francoise Couillard, baptized 1695 Montmagny, joined a religious order.

V-vi.   Marie-Simone, baptized 1697 Montmagny, married 1719 Alexis-Jean Guyon.

V-vii.   Francois Couillard, born 22
          Nov. 1699 Montmagny,
          married 1728 Madeleine
          Bernier.
V-viii.   Joseph Couillard, born 17
          Sept. 1701 Montmagny,
          married 1725 Marie-Marthe
          Belanger.
V-ix.   Jean-Baptiste-Charles
          Couillard, born 11 July 1703
          Montmangy, married 1729
          Genevieve Langlois.
V-x.   Catherine Couillard, born 3
          April 1705 Montmagny, died
          1706.
V-xi.   Paul Couillard, born 8 Sept.
          1707 Montmagny.

The children of Louis and Louise
(Generation V):
V-i.   Antoine Couillard, baptized
          1719.
V-ii.   Marie-Anne Couillard,
          baptized 1721.
V-iii.   Louis Couillard, baptized
          1723.
IV-v. Genevieve Couillard, born 23 Oct.
       1660 Quebec, married 27 Sept. 1686,
       Pierre Denis.
       The child of Genevieve and Pierre
       (Generation V):
       V-i.   Charles Denis, born 24 July
                 1687 Quebec, died in August.
IV-vi. Jacques Couillard, born 5 June 1665
       Quebec, married 21 Jan. 1691
       Elisabeth Lemieux, daughter of
       Guillaume Lemieux and Elisabeth
       Langlois. Elisabeth was a midwife. She
       was elected by popular vote to the

Women's Assembly in the parish in
1703.
The children of Jacques and Elisabeth,
all of whom were born in Montmagny
(Generation V):

V-i.   Marie Couillard, born 8 Jan
          1692, married 1711 Jean-
          Francois Chorel.

V-ii.   Elisabeth Couillard, born 30
          March 1694, married 1716
          Bernard Damours.

V-iii.   Jacques Couillard, baptized
          1696, married 1723 Marie-
          Louise Boulay.

V-iv.   Marthe Couillard, baptized
          1698, married 1716 Pierre
          Belanger.

V-v.   Augustin Couillard, born 25
          Dec. 1699, died 1721.

V-vi.   Joseph Couillard, born 24
          Oct. 1701.

V-vii.   Louise-Angelique Couillard,
          born 21 March 1704.

V-viii.   Jean-Baptiste Couillard, born
          26 Dec. 1705.

V-ix.   Louis Couillard, born 1 Sept.
          1707, died 1710.

V-x.   Marie-Madeleine Couillard,
          born 17 May 1710, married
          1728 Charles Couillard.

V-xi.   Clement Couillard, born 20
          Oct. 1712.

V-xii.   Louis Couillard, 3 Sept.
          1714.

III-iv. Elisabeth Couillard, born 9 Feb. 1631 Quebec,
         married 27 Nov. 1645 Jean Guyon, son of Jean
         Guyon and Mathurine Robin. Jean was a
         surveyor for the king.

The children of Elisabeth and Jean (Generation IV):

IV-i.   Marie-Madeleine Guyon, born 23 Aug. 1647 Quebec, married 24 Nov. 1661 Adrien Hayot, son of Thomas Hayot and Jeanne Boucher.
The children of Marie-Madeleine and Adrien (Generation V):

    V-i.   Marie-Anne Hayot, born 5 March 1663 Chateau-Richer, married 1681 Jean Marchand.

    V-ii.   Anne Hayot, born 1665, died 1690 Tilly.

    V-iii.   Charles Hayot, born ca. 1667.

    V-iv.   Adrien Hayot, born 2 April 1669 L'Ange-Gardien, died 1712.

    V-v.   Louis Hayot, born 23 April 1671 L'Ange-Gardien, married 1693 Marie-Louise Gourault.

    V-vi.   Joseph Hayot, born 15 March 1673, died in April.

    V-vii.   Francois Hayot, born 3 June 1674 Chateau-Richer.

IV-ii.   Joseph Guyon, born 10 Sept. 1649 Quebec, married 29 Jan. 1674 Chateau-Richer, Genevieve Cloutier, daughter of Zacharie and Madeleine Emard.
The children of Joseph and Genevieve (Generation V):

    V-i.   Madeleine Guyon, born 15 Dec. 1674 Chateau-Richer, married 1692 Antoine Goulet.

V-ii.   Angelique Guyon, born ca.
           1677, married 1694 Jacques
           Letourneau.

V-iii.   Ignace Guyon, born 13 Feb.
           1680 L'Ange-Gardien,
           married 1705 Marie-Louise
           Guillet.

V-iv.   Joseph Guyon, born 27 April
           1682 L'Ange-Gardien,
           married 1710 Elisabeth
           Guillet.

V-v.   Jean-Baptiste Guyon, born 21
           Oct. 1684 L'Ange-Gardien,
           married 1718 Marie-Jeanne
           Guillet.

V-vi.   Charles Guyon, born 18
           March 1686 L'Ange-
           Gardien.

V-vii.   Noel Guyon, born 5 Sept.
           1688 L'Ange-Gardien, died
           1692.

V-viii.   Ambroise Guyon, born 5 Jan.
           1690 L'Ange-Gardien, died
           1692.

V-ix.   Marie-Madeleine Guyon,
           born 1693 La Perade, died
           1714 Grodines.

V-x.   Genevieve Guyon, born 23
           May 1696 La Perade.

IV-iii. Francois-Xavier Guyon, born 15 Oct.
         1651 Quebec, married 14 July 1683
         Chateau-Richer, Marie Clotus,
         daughter of Abraham Clotus and Marie
         Dumont of Paris.
         The children of Francoise and Marie
         (Generation V):

V-i.   Francois Guyon, born 12
           April 1684 Cap St. Ignace,

	died the 30th.
V-ii.	Jean-Francois Guyon, born 14 Feb. 1685 L'Islet.
V-iii.	Marie Guyon, born ca. 1687, married 1705 Nicolas Gamache.
V-iv.	Joachim Guyon, born 1689 Cap St. Ignace, died 1710 L'Islet.
V-v.	Marguerite Guyon, baptized 1690 Cap St. Ignace, married 1711 Augustin Gamache.
V-vi.	Joseph Guyon, born 6 Jan 1693 Cap St. Ignace, died the 20th.
V-vii.	Jean Guyon, born 25 Feb. 1694 Cap St. Ignace, died March.
V-viii.	Francois Guyon, born 2 March 1695 Cap St. Ignace, died the 15th.
V-ix.	Noel Guyon, born 20 Aug. 1698 Cap St. Ignace, died the 22nd.
IV-iv.	Guillaume Guyon, born 17 Nov. 1652 Quebec, married 3 Nov. 1688 Jeanne Toupin, daughter of Toussaint Toupin and Marie Bourdon

The children of Guillaume and Jeanne (Generation V):

V-i.	Jean-Baptiste Guyon, born 5 Aug. 1690 Chateau Richer, married 1711 Marie Trudel.
V-ii.	Elisabeth-Ursule Guyon, born 28 Nov. 1691 Chateau Richer, died 1692.
V-iii.	Paul Guyon, born 3 May 1693 Chateau Richer.

V-iv.   Guillaume Guyon, born 15
        Sept. 1695 Chateau Richer,
        married 1730 Marie-Anne
        Masson.
V-v.   Marguerite Guyon, born 10
        Aug. 1697 Chateau Richer,
        died the 18th.
V-vi.   Joachim Guyon, born 23 Oct.
        1698 Chateau Richer,
        married 1727 Elisabeth-
        Agnes Morin.
V-vii. Marie-Francoise Guyon, born
        26 March 1700 Chateau
        Richer, died 1702.
V-viii. Pierre Guyon, born 14 March
        1702 Chateau Richer.
V-ix.   Augustin Guyon, born 16
        Jan. 1704 Chateau Richer.
V-x.   Nicolas Guyon, born 28 June
        1707 Chateau Richer, died
        1709.

IV-v.   Nicolas Guyon, born 13 Feb. 1655
        Quebec.
IV-vi. Jean-Francois Guyon, born 1 June
        1658 Quebec, died 1676.
IV-vii. Catherine-Gertrude Guyon, born 10
        Aug. 1660 Quebec, married 21 May
        1682 Denis Belleperche, son of Denis
        Belleperche and Antoinette Hebon of
        Picardy.
        The children of Catherine and Denis
        (Generation V):
        V-i.   Jean-Baptiste Belleperche,
                born 5 June 1683.
        V-ii.   Marguerite Belleperche, born
                ca. 1684.
        V-iii. Elisabeth Belleperche, born
                12 March 1686 Lauzon,

married 1718 Francois Petit.

V-iv.   Etienne Belleperche, born 28 Dec. 1687 Quebec.

V-v.   Marie-Anne Belleperche, born 17 May 1690 Quebec.

V-vi.   Catherine Belleperche, born 20 March 1694 Beaumont.

V-vii.   Catherine-Gertrude Belleperche, born 9 Nov. 1696 Quebec, died the 28th.

V-viii.   Pierre Belleperche, born 14 Sept. 1699 Quebec, married 1727 Angelique Esteve.

V-ix.   Claude Belleperche, born 24 Nov. 1702 Quebec, died 1704.

IV-viii. Marie Guyon, born 3 Sept. 1662 Quebec.

IV-ix. Genevieve Guyon, born 24 May 1665 Chaeau-Richer, married 8 Jan. 1690 Nicolas Doyon, son of Jean Doyon and Marthe Gagnon. Nicolas was a metalworker and made arquebusses (heavy match-lock gun; blunderbuss), armor, and locks.

V-i.   Jean Doyon, born 26 April 1691 Quebec, died same year.

V-ii.   a son, born and died 1692.

V-iii.   Nicolas Doyon, born and died 1693.

V-iv.   Ignace-Prisque Doyon, born and died 1694.

V-v.   Genevieve Doyon, born 6 Sept. 1695 Quebec, married 1716 Charles Hedoin.

V-vi.   Marie-Charlotte Doyon, born 1 Sept. 1696 Quebec, died 1700.

V-vii.   Marguerite Doyon, born 13 March 1699 Quebec.

V-viii.   Charles Doyon, born 3 March 1701 Quebec, died the 20th.

V-ix.   Marie-Angelique Doyon, born and died 1702.

V-x.   Louise Doyon, born 2 June 1703 Quebec, married 1721 Jean Beaudry.

V-xi.   Nicolas Doyon, born 14 May 1705 Quebec.

V-xii.   Louis Doyon, born and died 1707.

V-xiii.   Marie-Charlotte Doyon, born 10 Sept. 1708.

V-xiv.   Elisabeth Doyon, born and died 1712.

IV-x.   Charles Guyon, born 27 Sept. 1667 Chateau-Richer, a twin, died before 1681.

IV-xi.   Elisabeth Guyon, born 27 Sept. 1667 Chateau-Richer, a twin, died before 1681.

IV-xii.   Pierre Guyon, born 18 July 1670 Chateau-Richer, married 11 Oct. 1694 L'Ange-Gardien, Angelique Tetu, called Dutilly, daughter of Pierre Tetu and Genevieve Rigaud.

The children of Pierre and Angelique (Generation V):

V-i.   Jean-Baptiste Guyon, born 22 June 1696 Chateau Richer, married 1723 Marie-Catherine Tetreau.

V-ii.   Louis Guyon, born 16 Sept.

1697 Chateau Richer,
married 1722 Marie
Gamache.

IV-xiii. Ange Guyon, born 15 May 1674
Chateau-Richer, died before 1681.

III-v. Marie Couillard, baptized 1633 Quebec,
married 25 Oct. 1648 Francois Bissot, son of
Jean Bissot and Marie Assour of the province
of Normandy, France.
The children of Marie and Francois
(Generation IV):

IV-i.   Jean-Francois Bissot, born 6 Dec. 1649
Quebec, died 1663.

IV-ii. Louise Bissot, born 15 Sept. 1651
Quebec, married 12 Aug. 1668
Seraphyin Margane, son of Sebastien
Margane and Denise Fonnot of Paris,
France. Seraphyin was a military man.
The children of Louise and Seraphyin
(Generation V):

V-i.   Marie-Anne Margane, born
19 June 1668 Quebec,
married 1694 Ignace
Boucher.

V-ii.   Charles-Seraphin Margane,
baptized 1669 Montreal,
killed by the Iroquois 1693.

V-iii. Francois-Marie Margane,
born 29 Oct. 1672 Montreal,
killed in Deerfield, Mass.,
1704.

V-iv.   Genevieve Margane, born 1
Nov. 1674 Monreal, married
1696 Charles LeGardeur.

V-v.   Madeleine-Louise Margane,
born 27 Nov. 1676 Lavaltrie,
married 1698 Paul
d'Ailleoust.

V-vi.   Pierre-Paul Margane, born
          ca. 1678.
V-vii.   Barbe Margane, 18 Dec.
          1680, married 1719 Etienne
          de Bragelone.
V-viii.   Jean-Baptiste Margane, born
          3 Nov. 1683 Lavaltrie.
V-ix.   Francois Margane, born 9
          Sept. 1685, married 1712
          Angelique Guyon.
V-x.   Catherine-Alphonsine
          Margane, born and died
          1690.
V-xi.   Louise-Marguerite Margane,
          baptized 1691 Montreal,
          married 1713 Claude-Charles
          DuTisne.

IV-iii. Genevieve Bissot, baptized 1653
         Quebec, married 12 June 1673 Quebec,
         Louis Maheu, son of Rene Maheu and
         Marguerite Corriveau. Louis was a
         surgeon, a merchant in the lower
         village of Quebec, and the first captain
         of the port of Quebec.
         The children of Genevieve and Louis
         (Generation V):
         V-i.   Louis-Francois Maheu, born
                  1684 Quebec, died 1685.
                  Genevieve had a child with
                  Nicolas Daneau de Muy; a
                  son, Nicolas, born 1687
                  Lauzon.

IV-iv.   Catherine Bissot, born 6 March 1655
         Quebec, married 27 Nov. 1670
         Lauzon, Etienne Charet, son of Pierre
         Charet and Renee Merle of the
         province of Poitou, France.
         The children of Catherine Bissot and

Etienne (Generation V):

V-i.   Marie-Charlotte Charet, born
       31 Dec. 1671 Lauzon,
       married 1687 Pierre-Gratien
       Martel.

V-ii. Marie-Ursule Charet, born
       and died 1673.

V-iii. Francoise Charet, born 4
       March 1674 Lauzon, married
       1692 Rene Boucher.

V-iv. Genevieve Charet, born 1676
       Lauzon.

V-v.   Etienne Charet, born 1678
       Lauzon, married 1713 Anne-
       Therese Duroy.

V-vi. Marie Charet, born ca. 1679,
       died 1690 Lauzon.

V-vii. Catherine Charet, born 1681
       Lauzon, married 1699 Pierre
       Trottier.

V-viii. Jean-Baptiste Charet, born 4
       April 1683 Lauzon, married
       1714 Louise Allemand.

V-ix. Joseph-Alexis Charet, born
       ca. 1685, became a priest.

V-x.   Pierre Charet, born 29 Aug.
       1688 Lauzon, became a
       priest.

V-xi. Marie-Madeleine Charet,
       born 20 Sept. 1690 Lauzon,
       died 1691.

V-xii. Marie-Ursule, born 4 May
       1692 Lauzon, died 1720.

IV-v. Claire-Francoise Bissot, born 13 April
      1656 Quebec, married 7 Oct. 1675
      Quebec, Louis Jolliet, son of Jean
      Jolliet and Marie d'Abancourt. Louis
      left the seminary to become a

merchant, explorer (1668-1673 in the West), and a fisherman off Labrador. The children of Claire-Francoise and Louis (Generation V):

V-i.   Louis Jolliet, born 11 Aug. 1676 Quebec, died ca. 1709 in LaRochelle.

V-ii.   Charles-Marie Jolliet, born 12 June 1678 Quebec, married 1714 Jeanne Lemelin.

V-iii. Francois Jolliet, born 1 Oct. 1679 Quebec, died before 1725.

V-iv.   Marie-Genevieve Jolliet, born 1681 L'Islet, married 1696 Jean Grignon.

V-v.   Jean-Baptiste Jolliet, born 10 May 1683 Quebec, married 1708 Marie Mars.

V-vi.   Claire Jolliet, born 6 March 1685 Quebec, married 1702 Joseph Fleury. She inherited the estates of her brothers Louis and Francois.

IV-vi. Marie Bissot, born 3 July 1657 Quebec, married 5 Dec. 1682 Quebec, Claude Porlier, son of Claude Porlier and Marie Filerain of Paris, France. Claude was a merchant. The children of Marie and Claude (Generation V):

V-i.   Claude-Cyprien Porlier, born 6 Oct. 1683 Quebec, married 1719 Angelique Cuillerier.

V-ii.   Jean-Baptiste Porlier, born 23 Oct. 1685 Quebec, married in Port Royal, Acadia, Marie-

> Anne de Saint Etienne de
> LaTour.

V-iii.   Henri-Francois Porlier, born
13 Jan 1687 Quebec, died
before 1716.

IV-vii. Guillaume Bissot, born 16 Sept. 1661
Quebec, died before 1681.

IV-viii. Charles-Francois Bissot, born 5 Feb.
1664 Quebec, married 28 Feb. 1699
Anne-Francoise Forestier, daughter of
Antoine Forestier and Marie-
Madeleine Cavelier.

The child of Charles and Anne (Generation V):

V-i.   Marie-Madeleine Bissot,
born 1699 Montreal.

IV-ix.   Charlotte Bissot, born 4 June 1666
Quebec, married 1686 Pierre Benac.
They did not have children.

IV-x.   Jean-Baptiste Bissot, born 19 Jan. 1668
Quebec, married 19 Sept. 1696
Montreal, Marguerite Forestier,
daughter of Antoine Forestier and
Marie-Madeleine Cavelier. Jean was a
post commandant in present-day
Indiana area.

The children of Jean and Marguerite
(Generation V):

V-i.   Marie-Louise Bissot, born 21
June 1697 Montreal.

V-ii.   Clare-Charlotte Bissot, born
6 May 1698 Quebec, joined a
religious order.

V-iii.   Francois-Marie Bissot, born
17 June 1700 Montreal.

V-iv.   Marguerite-Catherine Bissot,
born 10 Sept. 1701 Montreal.

V-v.   Angelique Bissot, born ca.
1702, died 1718 Lachine.

            V-vi.   Catherine Bissot, born 11 Oct. 1704 Montreal.

            V-vii.   Michel Bissot, baptized 19 Oct. 1706 Trois Rivieres, died 1709 Montreal.

            V-viii.   Pierre Bissot, born and died 1710 Montreal.

IV-xi.   Jeanne Bissot, born 11 April 1671 Quebec, married 7 April 1687 Quebec, Philippe Clement, son of Antoine Clement and Francoise de Coeur of the province of Picardy, France.

The children of Jeanne and Philippe (Generation V):

            V-i.   Francois-Philippe Clement, born 10 June 1691 Quebec.

            V-ii.   Jean Clement, born 6 June 1694 Quebec, died in October.

IV-xii.   Francois-Joseph Bissot, born 19 May 1673 Quebec, married 4 Feb. 1698 Quebec, Marie Lambert. Francois was a merchant and navigator.

The children of Francois and Marie (Generation V):

            V-i.   Louise-Claire Bissot, baptized 1701 Quebec, married 1726 Jean Fournel.

            V-ii.   Charlotte Bissot, born 30 April 1704 Quebec, married 1728 Jacques de Lafontaine.

            V-iii.   Francois-Etienne Bissot, born 25 May 1708 Quebec, died 1726.

            V-iv.   Claire Bissot, born 1709, died 1710.

            V-v.   Jean Bissot, born and died 1711 Quebec.

V-vi.   Joseph Bissot, born and died
          1713.
V-vii.   Marie Bissot, born 1715
          Mingan, died 1720 Quebec.
V-viii.   Louise Bissot, born 1718
          Quebec, died 1730.
V-ix.   Angelique Bissot, born 12
          Dec. 1719 Quebec.
V-x.   Marie-Charlotte Bissot, born
          1722 Mingan.

III-vi. Guillaume Couillard, baptized 1635 Quebec,
         killed by the Iroquois near Tadoussac ca. 1662.
III-vii. Madeleine Couillard, baptized 1639 Quebec,
         died before 1666.
III-viii. Nicolas Couillard, baptized 1641 Quebec, died
         1661 Quebec, killed by the Iroquois.
III-ix. Charles Couillard, born 10 May 1647 Quebec,
         married 10 Jan. 1668 Quebec, Marie Pasquier
         de Franclieu, daughter of Pierre Pasquier and
         Marie de Porta of Paris, France. Marie died in
         1685. Charles married 25 June 1686 Metru
         (Lauzon), Louise Couture, daughter of
         Guillaume Couture and Anne Emard/Aymard.
         The children of Charles and Marie (Generation
         IV):
         IV-i.   Marie-Guillemette Couillard, born and
                   died 1669 Quebec.
         IV-ii.   a son, born and died 1670 Quebec.
         IV-iii.   Charles Couillard, born and died 1671
                   Quebec.
         IV-iv.   a son, born and died 1672 Quebec.
         IV-v.   a son, born and died 1673 Quebec.
         IV-vi.   Charles-Marie Couillard, born 28
                   March 1675 Lauzon, married 13 May
                   1726 Beaumont, Marie-Francoise
                   Couture, called Bellerive, daughter of
                   Eustache Couture and Marie-Francoise
                   Huard.

The children of Charles-Marie and
Marie-Francoise (Generation V):
V-i.   Charles Couillard, born and
            died 1727 Beaumont.
V-ii.   Marie-Francoise Couillard,
            born 4 Feb. 1728 Beaumont,
            married 6 Nov. 1758 Louis
            Turgeon.
V-iii.   Marie-Josephe Couillard,
            born 9 Dec. 1730 Beaumont,
            died 1744.
V-iv.   Charles Couillard, born 2
            May 1733 Beaumont,
            married 7 Jan. 1757 Marie-
            Francoise Boilard.
V-v.   Marie-Louise Couillard, born
            and died 1733 Beaumont.
V-vi.   Catherine Couillard, born
            1735 Beaumont, died 1736.
V-vii.   Catherine Couillard, born and
            died 1737.
V-viii.   Etienne Couillard, born and
            died 1740.
The children of Charles and Louise
(Generation IV):
IV-i.   Louis Couillard, born and died 1687
            Lauzon.
IV-ii.   Jeanne Couillard, born and died 1688
            Lauzon.
IV-iii.   Louise Couillard, born ca. 1689, died
            1692 Lauzon.
IV-iv.   Philippe Couillard, born 19 April 1691
            Lauzon, died 1698 Beaumont.
IV-v.   Joseph Couillard, born 27 May 1693
            Beaumont, married 8 Aug. 1729
            Beaumont, Genevieve Turgeon,
            daughter of Zacharie Turgeon and
            Elisabeth Roy.

The children of Joseph and Genevieve (Generation V):

V-i.   Genevieve Couillard, born 30 Oct. 1730 Beaumont.

V-ii.   Joseph Couillard, baptized 1732 Beaumont, died 1737.

V-iii.   Charles Couillard, born and died 1733 Beaumont.

V-iv.   Marie-Genevieve Couillard, baptized 1734 Beaumont, married 1753 Joseph Alaire.

V-v.   Marguerite Couillard, baptized 1736 Beaumont, married 1761 Jean Guay.

V-vi.   Joseph Couillard, baptized 24 March 1738 Beaumont, married 1763 Madeleine Filteau.

V-vii.   Marie-Louise Couillard, born 1740, died 1757.

V-viii.   Marie-Joseph Couillard, born 1742, died 1744.

V-ix.   Cecile Couillard, baptized 1745, married 1766 Thomas Guenet.

V-x.   Marie-Joseph Couillard, born 1748, died 1754.

V-xi.   Marie-Francoise, baptized 1751 Beaumont, married Louis Alaire.

V-xii.   Marie Couillard married Jean-Baptiste Gosselin.

IV-vi. Charles Couillard, born 13 Aug. 1695 Beaumont, married 20 Oct. 1728 Montmagny, Madeleine Couillard, called Despres, daughter of Jacques Couillard and Elisabeth Lemieux.

The children of Charles and Madeleine (Generation V):

V-i.   Madeleine-Catherine Couillard, born and died 1730 Beaumont.

V-ii.   Charles Couillard, born 1731, died 1733.

V-iii.   Louis-Joseph Couillard, born and died 1733.

V-iv.   Marie-Madeleine Couillard, born and died 1734.

V-v.   Charles Couillard, born 1735, married 1761 Veronique Cote.

V-vi.   Marie-Madeleine Couillard, born 1737, married 1755 Jacques Joncas.

V-vii.   Louise Couillard, born 1738, married 1760 Louis Joncas.

V-viii. Louis-Francois Couillard, born and died 1740.

V-ix.   Louis Couillard, born and died 1742.

V-x.   Robert Couillard, born and died 1744.

V-xi.   Roger Couillard, born and died 1746.

V-xii.   Joseph Couillard, born and died 1748.

IV-vii. Marie Couillard, born 18 Nov. 1697 Beaumont, married 21 Feb. 1724 Alexandre Morel, son of Louis-Joseph Morel and Elisabeth Rame.

The children of Marie and Alexandre (Generation V):

V-i.   Charles Morel, born and died 1725 Beaumont.

V-ii.   Marie-Francoise Morel, born

1726 La Durantaye.

V-iii.   Charles-Joseph Morel, born
16 Feb. 1728 Beaumont.

V-iv.   Marguerite Morel, born and
died 1729 Beaumont.

V-v.   Madeleine-Regis Morel, born
13 Nov. 1730 Beaumont,
married 1752 Thomas
Fournier.

V-vi.   Jean-Baptiste Morel, born
1732.

V-vii.   Cecile Morel, born 1734,
married 1760 Nicolas-
Charles-Louis Levesque.

V-viii.   Joseph Morel, born 1736.

IV-viii. Marie-Louise Couillard, born 8 April
1700 Beaumont, died 1725.

IV-ix.   Pierre Couillard, born and died 1702
Beaumont.

IV-x.   Marie-Anne Couillard, born 16 May
1703 Beaumont, a twin, married 11
Feb. 1727 Beaumont Jean-Baptiste
Girard, son of Jacques Girard and
Mathurine Poire.
The children of Marie-Anne and Jean-
Baptiste (Generation V):

V-i.   Genevieve Girard, born 22
Feb. 1728 Beaumont, married
1749 Francois Berlinguet.

V-ii.   Jean-Baptiste Girard, born
1729 Beaumont, died 1730.

V-iii.   Charles-Francois Girard,
born 1731, married 1750
Marie-Joseph Roy.

V-iv.   Therese Girard, born 1735.

V-v.   Marie-Charlotte Girard, born
1737, married 1756 Nicolas
Boilard.

V-vi.   Marie-Francoise Girard, born
         and died 1739.

V-vii.   Elisabeth-Joseph Girard, born
         and died 1744.

IV-xi. Pierre Couillard, born 16 May 1703
        Beaumont, a twin, married 22 July
        1727 Beaumont, Elisabeth Nadeau,
        daughter of Jean-Baptiste Nadeau and
        Anne Casse.
        The children of Pierre and Elisabeth
        (Generation V):

V-i.   Francois Couillard, born
         1728, married 1756, Marie-
         Joseph Moleur.

V-ii.   Elisabeth Couillard, born
         1730 Beaumont, married
         1761 Maruice Jean; married
         1762 Andre Noreau.

V-iii.   Marie-Anne Couillard, born
         1733, married 1753 Jean-
         Baptiste Guenet.

V-iv.   Marie-Francoise Couillard,
         born and died 1734.

V-v.   Marie-Genevieve Couillard,
         born 1737.

V-vi.   Marie-Louise Couillard, born
         1739.

V-vii.   Pierre Couillard, born and
         died 1741.

V-viii. Genevieve Couillard, born
         1743, died 1750.

V-ix.   a child, born and died 1745.

V-x.   Francoise-Elisabeth, born and
         died 1747.

V-xi.   a child, born and died 1749.

IV-xii. Marguerite Couillard, baptized 1707
        Beaumont, married 7 Nov. 1726
        Joseph Cote, son of Louis Cote and

Genevieve Bernier.

The children of Marguerite and Joseph (Generation V):

V-i.   Joseph Cote, born 2 Aug. 1727 Montmagny, died 1733.

V-ii.   Louis Cote, born 25 March 1729 Montmagny.

V-iii. Marguerite Cote, married 1749 Joseph Bouchard.

V-iv.   Joseph Cote, married 1771 Angelique Laberge.

III-x. Catherine-Gertrude Couillard, born 21 Sept. 1648 Quebec, married 6 Feb. 1664 Quebec, Charles Aubert, son of Jacques Aubert and Marie Goupy of the province of Picardy, France.

The child of Catherine and Charles (Generation IV):

IV-i.   Charles Aubert, born 17 Nov. 1664 Quebec, died in combat in France between 1690 and 1693.

II-iii. Anne Hebert married 1618 Etienne Jonquest. Anne died in 1619 or 1620 in childbirth. There are no further records of the child.

The Juchereau Family

I. Jean Juchereau, son of Jean Juchereau and Jeanne Creste of the province of Perche, France, married before 1621 in France, Marie Langlois, whose parentage is unknown. Jean arrived in Quebec in 1634. He was given a land grant in 1635 by the Company of One Hundred Associates (Cent-Associes). He was a member of the Community of Habitants, the Conseil Souverain, and the council that oversaw the fur trade.

The children of Jean and Marie (Generation II):

II-i.   Jean Juchereau, born ca. 1621, married 1645 Marie-Francoise Giffard.

The children of Jean and Marie-Francoise (Generation III):
see Giffard Family.

II-ii.   Nicolas Juchereau, born ca. 1625 or 1626, married
         1649 Marie-Therese Giffard.

The children of Nicolas and Marie-Therese (Generation III):
see Giffard Family.

II-iii. Louis Juchereau, born and died in France.

II-iv.   Genevieve Juchereau, born in France, married 1 Oct.
         1648 Quebec, Charles LeGardeur, son of Rene
         Legardeur and Catherine de Corday, probably of
         Normandy, France. Charles was governor at Trois
         Rivieres from 1648 to 1650 and a member of the
         Community of Habitants and the Conseil Souverain.
         The children of Genevieve and Charles (Generation
         III):

III-i.   Catherine LeGardeur, born 9 Aug. 1649
           Sillery, married 1668 Pierre de Saurel.

III-ii.   Marie LeGardeur, born 10 Feb. 1651 Quebec,
           married 1672 Alexandre Berthier.

III-iii.   Pierre-Noel LeGardeur, born 1652 Sillery,
           married 1675 Marguerite Volant.

III-iv.   Jean-Baptiste LeGardeur, born 13 June 1655
           Quebec, died in Rochefort.

III-v.   Marguerite LeGardeur, born 29 July 1657
           Quebec, married 1694 Louis-Joseph LeGoues.

III-vi.   Charles LeGardeur, born 24 Aug. 1659
           Quebec, married 1696 Genevieve Margane.

III-vii.   Rene LeGardeur, born 3 Oct. 1660 Quebec,
           married 1694 Marie-Barbe de Saint-Ours.

III-viii. Marie-Madeleine LeGardeur, born 20 July
           1662 Quebec, joined a religious order.

III-ix.   Augustin LeGardeur, born 15 Oct. 1663
           Quebec, married in France.

III-x.   Genevieve-Gertrude LeGardeur, born 19 May
           1666 Quebec, married 1704 Jean-Baptiste
           Celoron.

III-xi.   Louise LeGardeur, born 28 Oct. 1667 Quebec,
           married 1689 Augustin Rouer.

III-xii. Jean-Baptiste LeGardeur, born 24 June 1669 Quebec, married 1697 Elisabeth Girard.

III-xiii. Charlotte-Francoise LeGardeur, born 8 Oct. 1670 Quebec, married 1689 Rene Damours.

III-xiv. Daniel LeGardeur, born 27 March 1672 Quebec, died 1694 Hudson Bay.

III-xv. Louise LeGardeur, born 24 March 1674 Quebec, married 1695 Louis de Gannes.

II-v. Francois Juchereau, born and died in France.

The Langlois Family

I. Noel Langlois, born ca. 1603, son of Guillaume Langlois and Jeanne Millet of the province of Normandy, France, married 1634 in Quebec Francoise Grenier/Garnier, whose origins are unknown. He was recruited by Robert Giffard to settle in the Beauport seigniory and was a pilot on The St. Lawrence River.

The children of Noel and Francoise (Generation II):

II-i. Robert Langlois, born 1635 Quebec, died 1654.

II-ii. Marie Langlois, born 1636 Quebec, died before 1666.

II-iii. Anne Langlois, born 1637 Quebec, married 9 Nov. 1649 Jean Pelletier/Peltier, called Gobloteur or LeGobloteur, son of Guillaume Pelletier and Michelle Mabille. He was a carpenter.

The children of Anne and Jean (Generation III):

III-i. Noel Pelletier, born 3 May 1654 Quebec, married 1674 Madeleine Mignault.

III-ii. Anne Pelletier, born 1 Oct. 1656 Quebec, married 1670 Guillaume Lizot.

III-iii. Rene Pelletier, born 2 March 1659 Quebec, married 1691 Marie-Madeleine Leclerc.

III-iv. Antoine Pelletier, born and died 1661 Quebec.

III-v. Jean Pelletier, born 19 April 1663 Quebec, married 1689 Marie-Anne Huot.

III-vi. Marie-Daphine Pelletier, born and died 1666.

III-vii. Marie Pelletier, born 4 May 1667 Ile d'Orleans, married 1686 Jacques Gerbert.

III-viii. Charles Pelletier, born 25 Sept. 1671 Beauport, married 1698 Marie-Therese Ouellet.

III-ix. Marie-Charlotte Pelletier, born 29 Sept. 1674 Beauport, married 1693 Andre Mignier.

II-iv. Marguerite Langlois, born 1639 Quebec, married 22 Oct. 1653 Quebec at the home of Jean Juchereau, Paul Vachon, son of Vincent Vachon and Sapience Rabeau of Poitou, France. Paul was a mason and a seigniorial notary.

The children of Marguerite and Paul (Generation III):

III-i. Paul Vachon, born 1656 Quebec, became a priest.

III-ii. Marguerite Vachon, born 1 Sept. 1658 Quebec, married 1675 Jean-Robert Duprac.

III-iii. Vincent Vachon, born 15 Feb. 1660 Quebec, married 1685 Louise Cadieux.

III-iv. Louise Vachon, born 25 May 1662 Beauport, married 1678 Leonard Paille.

III-v. Marie-Madeleine Vachon, born 13 Aug. 1664 Beauport, married 1681 Raphael Giroux.

III-vi. Marie-Charlotte Vachon, born 1666, died before 1681.

III-vii. Noel Vachon, born 12 Jan. 1669 Beauport, married 1695 Monique Giroux.

III-viii. Pierre Vachon, born 26 May 1671 Beauport, married 1696 Marie-Catherine Soulard.

III-ix. Anne-Therese Vachon, born 23 July 1674 Beauport, married 1691 Jean Turgeon.

III-x. Marie-Francoise Vachon, born ca. 1676, married 1698 Joseph-Francois Binet.

III-xi. Marie-Madeleine Vachon, born 8 Jan. 1680 Beauport, married 1699 Pierre Vallee.

III-xii. Guillaume Vachon, born 2 Dec. 1682 Beauport, died 1702.

II-v. Jean Langlois, called Boisverdun, born 1641 Quebec, married 19 Oct. 1665 Chateau Richer, Charlotte-Francoise Belanger, daughter of Francois Belanger and Marie Guyon.

The children of Jean and Charlotte-Francoise (Generation III):

III-i.   Jean-Francois Langlois (called Jean) born 27 Feb. 1667 Chateau Richer, married 1692 Genevieve Rousseau.

III-ii. Charles Langlois, born 1668, died before 1681.

III-iii. Marie Langlois, born and died 1670 Quebec.

III-iv. Genevieve Langlois, born 22 April 1672 Quebec, married 1690 Guillaume Levitre.

III-v.   Marie-Madeleine Langlois, born 1 June 1674 Ile d'Orleans, married 1691 Jean Leclerc.

III-vi. Elisabeth Langlois, born and died 1676.

III-vii. Pierre Langlois, born 18 Dec. 1677 Ile d'Orleans, married 1701 Marie-Angelique Baillargeon.

III-viii. Joseph Langlois, born 9 May 1680 Ile d'Orleans, married 1705 Louise Nolin.

III-ix. Clement Langlois, born 1682, Ile d'Orleans, married 1704 Marie-Anne Prevost.

III-x.   Elisabeth Langlois, born ca. 1684, married 1709 Francois Gagne.

III-xi. Paul Langlois, born 1684, found dead on the ice 1696 Ile d'Orleans.

II-vi. Jeanne Langlois, born 1643 Quebec, married 9 Jan. 1656 Quebec, Rene Chevalier, son of Rene Chevalier and Marie Lucre of Anjou, France. Rene was a master mason and a stone cutter.

The children of Jeanne and Rene (Generation III) (note that four of the children married members of the Parent family, all of whom were brothers and sister):

III-i.   Louise Chevalier, born 19 Oct. 1659 Quebec, married Jacques Parent.

III-ii. Francoise Chevalier, born and died 1661 Quebec.

III-iii. Jean Chevalier, born 18 Feb. 1663 Beauport, married 1686 Marguerite-Madeleine Avice.

III-iv. Guillaume Chevalier, born 3 May 1665 Beauport, married 1689 Jeanne Gauthier.

III-v.   Jacques Chevalier, born ca. 1667.

III-vi.   Michel Chevalier, born 22 Nov. 1670
        Beauport, married 1695 Charlotte Parent.

III-vii. Jeanne Chevalier, born 12 May 1673 Beauport,
        married 1692 Michel Parent.

III-viii. Marie-Therese Chevalier, born ca. 1675,
        married 1696 Etienne Parent.

II-vii. Elisabeth Langlois, born 1645 Quebec, married 6 Nov.
1662 Louis Cote, son of Jean Cote and Anne Martin.
The children of Elisabeth and Louis (Generation III):

III-i.   Marie-Madeleine Cote, born 18 Sept. 1663
        Chateau Richer, married 1682 Louis Lemieux.

III-ii.   Louis Cote, born 31 Jan. 1665 Chateau Richer,
        married 1691 Genevieve Bernier.

III-iii. Jean Cote, born 6 March 1667 Quebec, died
        1687 Chateau Richer.

II-viii. Marie Langlois, born 1646 Quebec, married 10 Aug.
1660 Francois Miville, called LeSuisse, son of Pierre
Miville and Charlotte Maugis.

III-i.   Francoise Miville, born 5 June 1663 Quebec,
        married 1680 Pierre Richard.

III-ii.   Marie Miville, born 30 March 1665 Quebec,
        married 1684 Michel Gosselin.

III-iii. Francois Miville, born 20 Feb. 1667 Lauzon.

III-iv.   Joseph Miville, born 8 June 1669 Quebec,
        married 1695 Genevieve Caron.

III-v.   Jeanne Miville, born 11 April 1671 Lauzon,
        married 1689 Denis Boucher.

III-vi.   Anne Miville, born 27 March 1673 Lauzon,
        married 1691 Mathurin Dube.

III-vii. Jacques Miville, born 27 April 1675 Lauzon,
        married 1706 Catherine Lecuyer.

III-viii. Jean-Baptiste Miville, born 27 June 1677
        Lauzon, died 1707 Montmagny.

III-ix.   Charles Miville, born 11 March 1679 Lauzon,
        married 1703 Marie Savaria.

III-x.   Jean-Francois Miville, born 1681, died 1703.

III-xi.   Angelique Miville, born 20 June 1683 Lauzon,

married 1702 Louis Gamache.

III-xii.   Pierre Miville, born ca. 1686, died 1688.

II-ix.   Jean Langlois (called Saint-Jean) born 1648 Quebec, married 5 Dec. 1675 Marie Cadieux, daughter of Charles Cadieux and Madeleine Macard.

The children of Jean and Marie (Generation III):

III-i.   Charles Langlois, born ca. 1676, died 1699.

III-ii.   Marie-Madeleine Langlois, born 20 Nov. 1678 Ile d'Orleans, married 1699 Jean Gagne.

III-iii.   Jean Langlois, born and died 1681.

III-iv.   Madeleine Langlois, born 28 Feb. 1682 Beauport, married 1700 Jean Blouin.

III-v.   Louis Langlois, born 18 Nov. 1684 Beauport, married 1708 Madeleine Guyon.

III-vi.   Francois Langlois, born 24 March 1690 Ile-aux-Grues, married 1718 Marie Genest.

II-x.   Noel Langlois, born 1651 Quebec, married 6 Jan. 1677 Aimee Caron, daughter of Robert Caron and Marie Crevet. Aimee died 4 Oct. 1685. Noel married 2 Dec. 1686 Beauport, Genevieve Parent, daughter of Pierre Parent and Jeanne Badeau.

The children of Noel and Aimee (Generation III):

III-i.   Francois Langlois, born 27 Oct. 1673 Beauport, married 1696 Jeanne Baugis.

III-ii.   Marie-Anne Langlois, born ca. 1675, married 1694 Jean Cote.

III-iii.   Madeleine-Louise Langlois, born 20 April 1680, died 1682.

III-iv.   Agnes Langlois, born 1682 Beauport, died 1683.

III-v.   Marie-Therese Langlois, born 31 May 1684 Beauport, died 1703.

The children of Noel and Genevieve (Generation III):

III-i.   Jean Langlois, born 15 July 1688 Beauport, married 1712 Marie-Madeleine Bisson.

III-ii.   Genevieve Langlois, born 30 July 1690 Beauport, married 1708 Rene Toupin.

III-iii.   Noel Langlois, born 22 Jan. 1692 Beauport,
           married 1721 Francoise Niquet.
III-iv.   Louise-Catherine Langlois, born 12 Sept. 1693
           Beauport, married 1714 Jean Huppe.

The Marsolet Family

I. Nicolas Marsolet, son of Nicolas Marsolet and Marguerite de
Planes of the province of Normandy, France, married 19
March 1637 in Normandy, Marie Barbier/LeBarbier, daughter
of Henri Barbier and Marie LeVillain of Rouen, Normandy.
Nicolas probably arrived in Quebec in 1613 with Champlain,
but could have returned to France and then to Canada in 1618.
Nicolas was a ship master, trader, clerk in the fur trade and
interpreter to the Montagnais and Algonquins. Champlain
disparaged Marsolet for the uncivilized lifestyle Marsolet
assumed while out in the wilds and for collaborating with the
Kirke brothers during the seizure of Quebec from 1629 to
1632. Marsolet was granted a seigniory and a number of fiefs,
but supposedly leased the land to farmers to clear and plant.
He was in contention with the Community of Habitants and
attempted to run his own trading trips for furs.
The children of Nicolas and Marie (Generation II):
II-i.   Marie Marsolet, baptized 1638 Quebec, married 30
         April 1652 Mathieu Damours, son of Louis Damours
         and Elisabeth Tessier of Paris, France.
         The children of Marie and Mathieu (Generation III):
         III-i.   Nicolas Damours, born and died 1653 Quebec.
         III-ii.   Louis Damours, born 16 May 1655 Quebec,
                   married 1686 Marguerite Guyon.
         III-iii. Mathieu Damours, born 14 March 1657
                   Quebec, married 1686 Louise Guyon.
         III-iv.   Elisabeth Damours, born 1 Dec. 1658 Quebec,
                   married 1684 Claude Charron.
         III-v.   Rene Damours, born 9 Aug. 1660 Quebec,
                   married 1689 Charlotte-Francoise LeGardeur.
         III-vi.   Charles Damours, born 4 March 1662 Quebec,
                   married 1688 Marie-Anne Genaple.
         III-vii. Joseph-Nicolas Damours, born 1664 Quebec,

died 1690.

III-viii. Claude-Louis Damours, born 18 Jan. 1666 Quebec, married 17 Jan. 1708 Port-Royal, Acadia, Anne Comeau.

III-ix. Bernard Damours, born 14 Dec. 1667 Quebec, married 1698 Marie-Jeanne leBorgne.

III-x. Daniel Damours, born and died 1669 Quebec.

III-xi. Madeleine Damours, born 1671 Quebec, died before 1681.

III-xii. Genevieve Damours, born 22 Aug. 1673 Quebec, married 1703 Jean-Baptiste Celoron.

III-xiii. Jacquette-Marie Damours, born 13 Oct. 1675 Quebec, married 1697 Etienne de Villedonne.

III-xiv. Marguerite Damours, born 30 Nov. 1677 Quebec, married 1698 Jacques Testard.

III-xv. Philippe Damours, born 6 Feb. 1680 Quebec, married 1722 Marie-Madeleine Menage.

II-ii. Louise Marsolet, baptized 1640 Quebec, married 20 Oct. 1653 Jean Lemire, son of Mathurin Lemire and Jeanne Vannier of Rouen, Normandy, France. Jean was a master carpenter.

The children of Louise and Jean (Generation III):

III-i. a son, born and died 1655 Quebec.

III-ii. a son, born and died 1657 Quebec.

III-iii. Jeanne-Elisabeth Lemire, born 13 June 1658 Quebec, married 1676 Pierre Glaumont.

III-iv. Marie, called Marie-Madeleine, Lemire, born 3 Feb. 1660 Quebec, married 1677 Pierre Moreau.

III-v. Joseph Lemire, born 6 March 1662 Quebec, married 1685 Anne Hedouin.

III-vi. Anne Lemire, born 13 March 1664 Quebec, married 1681 Laurent Tessier.

III-vii. Louise Lemire, born 10 May 1666 Quebec, married 1681 Pierre Pepin.

III-viii. Catherine-Eleonore Lemire, born 20 March 1668 Quebec, married 1686 Jean Raymond.

III-ix.   Marie-Anne Lemire, born 26 May 1669
          Quebec, married 1690 Gedeon de Catalogne.
III-x.   Jean Lemire, born 1671 Quebec, died before
          1681.
III-xi.   Charles Lemire, born and died 1673 Quebec.
III-xii. Marie-Charlotte Lemire born 1674, died 1677.
III-xiii. Jean-Francois Lemire, born 1675 Petite Riviere
          St. Charles, married 1701 Francoise Foucault.
III-xiv. Jean Lemire, born 5 Sept. 1676 Grande Allee,
          married 1703 Elisabeth Bareau.
III-xv.   Helene Lemire, born 28 Aug. 1678 Grande
          Allee, died 1681.
III-xvi. Pierre Lemire, born and died 1681 Quebec.
II-iii.   Joseph Marsolet, baptized 1642 Quebec, died before
          1666.
II-iv.   Genevieve Marsolet, born 10 Aug. 1644 Quebec,
          married 4 Sept. 1662 Michel Guyon, called
          Rouvray/DuRouvray, son of Jean Guyon and
          Mauthurine Robin.
The children of Genevieve and Michel (Generation III): See
II-viii in the Guyon Family.
II-v.   Madeleine Marsolet, baptized 1646 Quebec, married
          1662 Francois Guyon.
The children of Madeleine and Francois (Generation III): See
II-x in the Guyon Family.
II-vi.   Louis Marsolet, born 30 Sept. 1648 Quebec, died
          before 1666.
II-vii.   Jean Marsolet, born 20 April 1651 Quebec, married
          1680 Marguerite Couture. Their only child was born,
          died and was buried 27 March 1690 Quebec, and
          Marguerite died the day after. Jean married Marie-
          Anne Bolduc two months later, but they had no
          children.
II-viii. Anne Marsolet, born 1653 Quebec, died before 1666.
II-ix.   Elisabeth Marsolet, born 29 Sept. 1655 Quebec, died
          before 1666.
II-x.   Marie Marsolet, born ca. 1661, died 1677 Quebec.

The Martin Family

I. Abraham Martin, dit L'Ecossais (the Scot) for reasons
    unknown, married 1620 in France, Marguerite Langlois. The
    origins of neither Abraham nor Marguerite are known.
    Abraham and Marguerite arrived in Canada ca. 1620 with
    Marguerite's sister Francoise and her husband, Pierre
    Desportes. Abraham was known as a river pilot. He received
    two land grants, one of which is said to have included the
    Plains of Abraham in Quebec. He was said to be a close friend
    to Nicolas Marsolet, who was somewhat of a rebel in the
    colony. In 1649 Abraham was imprisoned on an accusation of
    improper conduct with a young girl. He died in 1664 at about
    age 75.

The children of Abraham and Marguerite (Generation II):

II-i.   Eustache Martin, one of the first children of European
        descent born in Canada, baptized 24 Oct. 1621 Quebec.
        (No record of marriage or offspring.)

II-ii. Marguerite Martin, baptized 1624 Quebec, married 22
        May 1638 Quebec, Etienne Racine, son of Rene Racine
        and Marie Loysel of Lisieux, Normandy, France.
        Etienne was a carpenter.

        The children of Marguerite and Etienne (Generation
        III):

        III-i.   a daughter, born and died 1640 Quebec.

        III-ii.   Louise Racine, baptized 1641 Quebec, married
                  1653 Simon Guyon.

        III-iii. Noel Racine, baptized 1643 Quebec, married
                  1667 Marguerite Gravel.

        III-iv.   Marie-Madeleine Racine, baptized 1746
                  Quebec, married 1661 Noel Simard.

        III-v.   Francois Racine, baptized 1649 Quebec,
                  married 1676 Marie Baucher.

        III-vi.   Marguerite Racine, baptized 1652 Quebec,
                  married 1667 Jean Gagnon.

        III-vii. Pierre Racine, baptized 1655 Quebec, married
                  1682 Louise Guyon.

        III-viii. Marie Racine, born ca. 1657, joined a religious
                  order.

III-ix.   Jeanne Racine, born ca. 1660, married 1682
        Jean Pare.

III-x.   Etienne Racine, baptized 1662 Chateau Richer,
        married 1683 Catherine Guyon.

II-iii.   Helene Martin, baptized 1627 Quebec, married 22 Oct.
1640 Quebec, Claude Etienne, son of Nicolas Etienne
and Alice de Beaumont of Lorraine, France. Helene
was a goddaughter of Samuel de Champlain. The only
child of Helene and Claude, Martin Etienne, was born
and died 1644 Quebec.

II-iv.   Marie Martin, baptized 1635 Quebec, married 21 Jan.
1648 Jean Cloutier, son of Zacharie Cloutier and Sainte
Dupont.

The children of Marie and Jean (Generation III): See II-ii of
the Cloutier Family.

II-v.   Adrien Martin, baptized 1638 Quebec.

II-vi.   Madeleine Martin, baptized 1640 Quebec, married 6
Feb. 1653 Quebec, Nicolas Forget/Froget, called
Despatis, son of Paul Forget and Nicole Chevalier of
the province of Normandy, France.

The children of Madeleine and Nicolas (Generation
III):

III-i.   Michel Forget, born and died 1656 Montreal.

III-ii.   Gabriel Forget, baptized 1659 Montreal, died
        before 1666.

III-iii.   Jacques Forget, baptized 1662 Montreal, died
        1728.

III-iv.   Marguerite Forget, baptized 1666 Montreal,
        married 1679 Jean Muloin.

III-v.   Louis Forget, baptized 1668 Montreal, married
        1688 Elisabeth Ethier.

III-vi.   Jean Forget, baptized 1671 Sorel, died before
        1681.

III-vii.   Guillaume Forget, born 3 Aug. 1674
        Lachenaie, married 1698 Barbe Beauchamp.

III-viii.   Jean-Baptiste Forget, born ca. 1679, married
        1700 Jeanne Beaudoin.

II-vii.   Barbe Martin, baptized 1643 Quebec, married 12 Jan.

1655 Pierre Biron, son of Jean Biron and Marie Razee of Poitou, France. The only child of Barbe and Pierre, Anne, was born 1660 Quebec and died before 1666.

II-viii. Anne Martin, baptized 1645 Quebec, married 12 Nov. 1658 Jacques Rate, son of Francois Rate and Jacquette Huguet of La Rochelle, Aunis, France.

The children of Anne and Jacques (Generation III):

III-i.   Jacques Rate, born and died 1659 Quebec.

III-ii.   Bertrand Rate, born and died 1660 Quebec.

III-iii.   Michel-Joseph Rate, born 1662 Quebec, died before 1666.

III-iv.   Marie-Anne Rate, born 13 Feb. 1665 Quebec, married 1683 Ignace Gosselin.

III-v.   Jean-Baptiste Rate, born 28 Dec. 1667 Isle d'Orleans, married 1698 Madeleine Blouard.

III-vi.   Anne Rate, born 16 Oct. 1670 Ile d'Orleans, married 1691 Jacques Trepanier.

III-vii. Jacques Rate, born 1673, died before 1681.

III-viii. Pierre Rate, born 11 Oct. 1675 Ile d'Orleans, married 1702 Jeanne Nolin.

III-ix.   Geneive Rate, born 27 Jan. 1678 Ile d'Orleans, married 1694 Jean Sicard.

III-x.   Louis Rate, born 17 June 1680 Ile d'Orleans, married 1700 Louis Martin.

III-xi.   Ignace Rate, baptized 1683 Ile d'Orleans, married 1705 Helene Bouchard.

III-xii. Guillaume Rate, born 14 Nov. 1686 Ile d'Orleans, married 1710 Marie Madeleine Nolin.

II-ix.   Charles-Amador Martin, born 6 March 1648 Quebec, became a priest.

The Nicolet Family

I. Jean Nicolet, born ca. 1598, son of Thomas Nicolet and Marie de Lamer of Cherbourg, Normandy, France, married 1637 in Quebec, Marguerite Couillard, daughter of Guillaume Couillard and Guillemette Hebert. Jean arrived in Canada in 1618 as an agent of the Compagnie des Marchands of Rouen

and Saint Malo. He served as an interpreter and liaison
between the French and the Hurons and Algonquins of
Allumette (Lark) Island from 1618 to 1620. He then spent
nine years among the Nipissings and had a lodge and store.
His log of native culture was used by Paul Le Jeune, a Jesuit,
in his reports called "Jesuit Relations," but the original log has
been lost. During his stay among the Nipissings, he and a
native woman had a daughter, who would have been one of
the first metis, or mixed blood, in Canada. In 1633 he
undertook an expedition to the 'China Sea," led by native
guides. He packed along a damask robe that was embroidered
with flowers and birds so as to be properly dressed when
presented the Chinese court. (The belief in a western water
route through North America to the Far East was still strong in
1633.) The elegant costume came in handy when he
encountered several tribes near Lake Michigan and negotiated
a peace and trade plans. Not finding the northern salt seaway
to China, he explored southward then returned to Quebec. He
became a clerk for the Compagnie des Cent-Associes at Trois
Rivieres, where he received a land grant with Olivier
Tardif/Letardif in 1637. Ironically, for all his back-country
travel, Jean drowned 27 Oct. 1642 near Sillery when the small
boat he was in overturned in the river during a hurried trip
back to Trois Rivieres to negotiate for the release of an
Iroquois prisoner.

The natural child of Jean and the Nipissirine:

II-i.   Madeleine, called Euphrosine, married 21 Nov. 1643
         Jean Leblanc, son of Clement Leblanc and Anne Fert
         or Jeanne Fevre of Normandy, France.
         The children of Madeleine and Jean (Generation III):
         III-i.   Jacques Leblanc, born 1648 Quebec, died
                   1669.
         III-ii.   Madeleine Leblanc, born 15 July 1652 Quebec,
                   married 1666 Jean Pichet.
         III-iii. a son, born and died 1654 Quebec.
         III-iv.   Marguerite Leblanc, born 25 May 1665
                   Quebec, died 1661.
         III-v.   Noel Leblanc, born and died 1660 Quebec.

The children of Jean and Marguerite (Generation II):
II-i.   Ignace Nicolet, born ca. 1640, died the same year.
II-ii.   Marguerite Nicolet, baptized Trois Rivieres, married 9
         July 1656 Quebec, Jean-Baptiste LeGardeur, son of
         Pierre LeGardeur and Marie Favery.
The children of Marguerite and Jean-Baptiste (Generation III):
See IV-ii of Hebert Family.

The Pinguet Family

I. Henri Pinguet, son of Noel Pinguet and Louise Lambert,
   married ca. 1612 in the province of Perche, France, Louise
   Lousche, daughter of Jean Lousche and Jeanne Lemoyne of
   Perche. Henri was a merchant. He arrived 31 May 1634 in
   Quebec with Robert Giffard. Henri was granted a fief near
   Quebec.
Of the eight children of Henri and Louise, five were born and
died in France. Three, born in France, married in Quebec
(Generation II):
II-i.   Francoise Pinguet, born 1625, married 7 Nov. 1645
         Quebec, Pierre Delaunay, son of Gilles Delaunay and
         Denise Dubois of the province of Maine, France. Pierre
         arrived in Quebec 1635 and was killed by the Iroquois
         1654.
         The children of Francoise and Pierre (Generation III):
         III-i.   Charles Delaunay, born 1648 Quebec, married
                   1695 Montreal, Marie-Anne Legras. Charles
                   worked for the Jesuits at a mission to the
                   Iroquois and was contracted in 1686 to explore
                   the West. He was also a merchant and a tanner.
         III-ii.   Louis Delaunay, born 1650 Quebec, married
                   1694 Marie-Catherine Aouacamgo.
         III-iii. Henri Delaunay, born 3 Feb. 1653 Quebec,
                   married 1679 Francoise Crete.
II-ii.   Noel Pinguet, born 1630, married 15 Oct. 1652
         Quebec, Marie-Madeleine Dupont, daughter of Jean
         Dupont and Marie Gauchet.
         The children of Noel and Marie-Madeleine (Generation
         III):

III-i.   Marie-Madeleine Pinguet, born 1653 Quebec, joined a religious order.

III-ii.   Jean Pinguet, born 1655 Quebec, became a priest.

III-iii. Pierre-Joseph Pinguet, born 15 Aug. 1658 Quebec, married 1689 Catherine Testard.

III-iv.   Marie-Anne Pinguet, born 18 Dec. 1660 Quebec, married 1681 Leonard Hazeur.

III-v.   Catherine Pinguet, born 1662 Quebec, joined a religious order.

III-vi.   Felix Pinguet, born and died 1665 Quebec.

III-vii. Nicolas Pinguet, born 25 Nov. 1666 Quebec, married Elisabeth de Peiras.

III-viii. Jacques Pinguet, born 27 Feb. 1668 Quebec, married 1691 Marie-Anne Morin.

III-ix.   Marie-Therese Pinguet, born and died 1671 Quebec.

III-x.   Charles Pinguet, born 8 Feb. 1673 Quebec, died before 1715.

III-xi.   Joseph-Denis Pinguet, born 23 Jan. 1675 Quebec, died 1720.

III-xii. Jeanne-Genevieve Pinguet, born and died 1676 Quebec.

II-iii. Pierre Pinguet, born 1631, married 4 Nov. 1659 Quebec, Anne Chevalier/Lechevalier of Saintonage, parentage unknown.

The children of Pierre and Anne (Generation III):

III-i.   Marie-Anne Pinguet, born 17 Oct. 1661 Quebec, married 1676 Isaac Hervieux.

III-ii.   Genevieve Pinguet, born 27 April 1665 Quebec, married 1682 Pierre Gatien.

III-iii. Louise Pinguet, born 27 Feb. 1668 Quebec, married 1687 Gaspard Petit.

III-iv.   Daniel Pinguet, born and died 1670 Quebec.

III-v.   Marie-Angelique Pinguet, born 12 March 1672, married 1688 Pierre Beaudin.

The Tardif/Letardif Family

I. Olivier Tardif/Letardif, born 1604 in the province of Brittany, France, married 3 Nov. 1637 Quebec, Louise Couillard, daughter of Guillaume Couillard and Guilemette Hebert. Louise died in 1641. Olivier married 16 May 1648 in La Rochelle, France, Barbe Aymart/Emard, sister-in-law of Zacharie Cloutier. Olivier was in Quebec from 1622 to 1629, returned to France during the Kirke brothers' occupation of Quebec, but crossed the Atlantic again in 1632. He was head clerk for the Compagnie des Cent-Associes in 1633, a judge of the court for the seigniory of Beaupre, and an interpreter for the Montagnais, Algonquin, and Huron languages. He stood as godfather to several natives and adopted three native children. He received a few land grants, including a portion of the seigniory at Beaupre in 1646, which he sold in 1662. He was said to have suffered premature senility and died in 1665 at Chateau Richer.

The child of Olivier and Louise (Generation II):

II-i.   Pierre Tardif, born 11 July 1641 Quebec, died between 1648 and 1666.

The children of Olivier and Barbe (Generation II):

II-i.   Barbe-Delphine Tardif, born 28 May 1649 Quebec, married 23 Nov. 1661 Chateau Richer, Jacques Cauchon, called Lamothe, son of Jean Cauchon and Jeanne Abraham.

The children of Barbe-Dalphine and Jacques (Generation III):

III-i.   Jacques-Baptiste Cauchon, born 4 May 1663 Chateau Richer, married 1689 Genevieve Plante.

III-ii.   Marie-Madeleine Cauchon, born 2 Dec. 1664 Chateau Richer, married 1690 Louis Michel.

III-iii. Jeanne Cauchon, born 18 oct. 1667 Chateau Richer, married 1689 Pierre Godin.

III-iv.   Anne Cauchon, born and died 1670 Chateau Richer.

III-v.   Anne Cauchon, born 11 Aug. 1671 Chateau Richer, joined a religious order.

III-vi.   Barbe Cauchon, born 20 Nov. 1673 Charteau
Richer, married 1709 Francois Marchand.

III-vii.   Antoine Cauchon, born 3 April 1675 Chateau
Richer, died before 1718.

III-viii.   Joseph Cauchon, born 16 May 1678 Chateau
Richer, married 1709 Marie Charrier.

III-ix.   Jean Cauchon, born 21 July 1680 Chateau
Richer, married 171 Anne Blouard.

III-x.   Genevieve Cauchon, born 17 Aug. 1682
Chateau Richer, married 1708 Joseph Huot.

III-xi.   Marie Cauchon, born 7 March 1685 Chateau
Richer, married 1724 Joseph Roger.

II-ii.   Charles Tardif, born 4 March 1652 Quebec.

II-iii. Guillaume Tardif, born 22 Oct. 1655 Quebec, married
16 April 1679 Louise Dubois, daughter of Pierre
Dubois and Francoise Meunier. Louise died before
1687. Guillaume married 28 April 1687 L'Ange-
Gardien, Marguerite Godin, daughter of Charles Godin
and Marie Boucher.

The children of Guillaume and Louise (Generation III):

III-i.   Guillaume Tardif, born 1680 St. Ignace.

III-ii.   Francoise Tardif, born 1682 St. Ignace, married
1712 Genevieve Giroux.

The children of Guillaume and Marguerite (Generation
III):

III-i.   Charles Tardif, born 4 June 1688 L'Ange-
Gardien, married 1716 Genevieve Roy.

III-ii.   Catherine Tardif, born and died 1690 L'Ange-
Gardien.

III-iii.   Marguerite Tardif, born 24 June 1691 L'Ange-
Gardien, married 1714 Louis Girard.

III-iv.   Angelique Tardif, born 6 Dec. 1693 L'Ange-
Gardien, maried 1714 Louis Trudel.

III-v.   Joseph Tardif, born 28 June 1696 L'Ange-
Gardien, married 1718 Marguerite Letartre.

III-vi.   Pierre Tardif, born 12 Oct. 1698 L'Ange-
Gardien, married 1722 Genevieve Blouin.

III-vii.   Barbe Tardif, born 22 Jan. 1701 L'Ange-

Gardien, married 1725 Nicolas Trudel, son of Pierre Trudel and Francoise Lefrancois.

III-viii. Claire Tardif, born 2 June 1703 L'Ange-Gardien, married 1728 Nicolas Trudel, son of Nicolas Trudel and Barbe Letartre.

III-ix. Veronique Tardif, born 4 Oct. 1705 L'Ange-Gardien.

APPENDIX V

Example of Pedigree, Modified Method, and
Full Reference Citations

This is a pedigree, modified method, showing the genealogical numbering system and full reference citations for the Rajotte-Duperre family genealogy, a direct line to the Hebert family of Quebec through the maternal line. No. 1 is the compiler. The father's number is twice that of the child. The mother's number is twice that of the child plus 1. (Personal information has been omitted for living persons.) Dates are written as day, month, year without commas.

Generation I:
1. Denise Mary Rajotte

Generation II:
2. Bruno Joseph Rajotte [occupation: machinist]
born: 3 July 1914 St. Germain, Quebec, Canada
married: 26 April 1947 Bristol, Conn.
died: 3 Oct. 2001 Bristol, Hartford, Conn.
3. Lucille Annette Duperre

Generation III:
4. Felix Rajotte [occupation: farmer, woodworker, fiddler]
born: 14 Dec. 1871 St. Germain de Grantham, Quebec, Canada
married: 8 Jan. 1895 St. Germain de Grantham
died: 10 April 1952 Bristol, Hartford, Conn.
5. (Marie) Exilda Bergeron
born: 13 Jan. 1875 Sorel, Quebec, Canada
died: 22 Jan. 1952 Bristol, Hartford, Conn.
6. Ubald H.P. Duperry / Henri Duperre [laborer; insurance agent, Prudential Co.]
born: 22 Sept. 1895 Fall River, Mass.
married: 23 June 1919 North Caribou, Aroostook, Maine
died: 13 Nov. 1974 Bristol, Hartford, Conn.
7. Bertha Levesque [domestic]

born: 1 Nov. 1900 New Sweden, Aroostook, Maine
died: 28 March 1967 Bristol, Hartford, Conn.

Generation IV:
8. Louis Rajotte
born: Canada
married: 16 Aug. 1859 Sorel, Quebec, Canada
9. Marie Bergeron
born: Canada
10. Felix Bergeron
born: Sorel, Quebec, Canada
married: 8 April 1872 Sorel, Quebec, Canada
11. Sophie Rajotte
born: Sorel, Quebec, Canada
12. Michel Duperry [occupation: weaver]
born: Canada
13. Marie Levesque
born : Canada – or –
born: Van Buren, Aroostook, Maine
died: 1 July 1933 Fairfield, Somerset, Maine
14. Thomas Levesque / Pierre Levesque / Peter Bishop
    [occupation: blacksmith]
born: Grand Falls, New Brunswick, Canada
married: 22 Jan. 1900
died: 18 July 1947 Stockholm, Aroostook, Maine
15. Jane Dasto / Jeanne Doustou / Jane Dastou
born: Edmundston, New Brunswick, Canada

Generation V:
16. Louis Rajotte
married: 14 Nov. 1826 Sorel, Quebec, Canada
17. Jeulie Lavallee
18. Ignace Bergeron [occupation: "cultivator," i.e., farmer]
19. Christine Ethier
20. Ignace Bergeron [occupation: "cultivator"]
21. Christine Ethier
22. Joseph Rajotte [occupation: "cultivator"]
23. Reine Paul-Hus

24. Michel Duperre
married: 12 Feb. 1854 Van Buren, Aroostock, Maine
25. Modeste Oulette
26. Jean-Baptiste Levesque
27. Basilise Lavoie
28. Maglore Levesque
born: Canada
29. Archange Landrais
born: Ft. Kent, Aroostook, Maine
30. Guillaume Dastous / William Daston
married: 12 Feb. 1877 St. David, New Brunswick, Canada
31: Apolline Ouelette

Generation VI:
32. Joseph Rajote (note spelling change)
married: 27 July 1795, Sorel, Quebec, Canada
33. Francoise Pizane

48. Joseph Dupere (note spelling change)
married: 30 Jan. 1826, Riviere du Loup, Quebec, Canada
49. Therese Fournier

Generation VII:
64. Jacques Rajot (note spelling change)
married: 9 Oct. 1752, Sorel, Quebec, Canada
65. Genevieve Hus

98. Pierre Fournier [occupation: "agriculteur"]
married: 3 Feb. 1801 St. Charles de Bellechasse, Quebec,
     Canada
99. Therese Labrecque

Generation VIII:
128. Francois Rageot (note spelling change) [occupation:
     "huissier, notaire royal de la prevote de cette ville" (Quebec);
     baillif, royal notary in Quebec]
married: 24 Nov. 1711 Quebec
129. Genevieve Gautier

196. Pierre Fournier
married: 2 Oct. 1769 Montmagny, Quebec, Canada
197. Marie Joseph Proux

Generation IX:
256. Gilles Rageot (origin: St. Jean L'aigle, eveche d'Evreux,
    Paris, France)
married: 29 May 1673 Quebec, Canada
257. Marie Madeleine Morin

392. Pierre Fournier
married: 3 Oct. 1743 Montmagny, Quebec, Canada
393. Marie Madeleine Morin

(Note that the Marie Madeleine Morin who married Gilles
    Rageot was not the same who married Pierre Fournier seventy
    years later, shown by the parentage of each.)

Generation X:
514. Noel Morin
married: 9 Jan. 1640 Quebec, Canada
515. Helene Desportes

784. Jean Fournier
married: 11 Feb. 1717 Montmagny, Quebec, Canada
785. Louise Jonca(s)
786. Joseph Morin
married: 4 Nov. 1704 Quebec, Canada
787. Marie-Anne Bridaut

Generation XI:
1568. Joseph Fournier
married: 25 June 1684
1569. Barbe Girard

Generation XII:
3136. Guillaume Fournier (origin: Normandy, France)
married: 20 Nov. 1651
3137. Francoise Hebert

Generation XIII:
6274. Guillaume Hebert
married: 1 Oct. 1634 Quebec
6275. Helene Desportes

(Note that Helene Desportes, Nos. 515 and 6275, is a link
between both maternal and paternal families. She married
Guillaume Hebert in 1634 and, after his death in 1639, married
Noel Morin in 1640.)

Generation XIV:
12,548. Louis Hebert (origin: Paris, France)
12,549. Marie Rollet
12,550. Pierre Desportes (origin: France)
12,551. Francoise Langlois

ENDNOTES

Following are the reference citations for the Rajotte-Duperre genealogy. Abbreviations used are: b. for born, d. for died, m. for married, o. for occupation, ditto for same as above. Documents were procured from municipal, state, province, national offices, or repositories. Information not available from documentation was obtained from reliable, well-known and accepted sources.

Pedigree charts have limited space that does not allow for full reference information. Numbered references follow the numbering system of the charts and serve as full citation endnotes. The format used is as described in the manual *Evidence!* by Elizabeth Shown Mills.

1. Denise Mary Rajotte, birth certificate no. 18786 (3-29-72), Connecticut State Department of Health — Local Registrar of Vital Statistics, Bristol.
2b. "Enlisted Record and Report of Separation Honorable Discharge," 30 Oct. 1945, Separation Center Ft. Devens, Mass.
2o. Marriage license, Connecticut State Department of Health, Bureau of Vital Statistics, Hartford, Conn., no. 142, Rolfe E. Rowe, Registrar.
2m. Marriage license, Connecticut State Department of Health, Bureau of Vital Statistics, Hartford, Conn., no. 142, Rolfe E. Rowe, Registrar.
2d. Bruno Rajotte, death certificate no. 534, Department of Public Health, Connecticut.
3b. Lucille Annette Duperre entry, Stockholm, Maine, births, No. 144, Town Clerk's Office.
4b. Church records, St. Germain de Grantham; B 92 Felise Rajotte. Archives nationales Quebec, Montreal.
4m. Registres d'etat civil 1888 a 1900, Protonotaire Drummond, St. Germain de Grantham; In 4 Felix Rajotte and Exilda Bergeron. Archives nationales Quebec, Montreal.
4d. Felix Rajotte, death certificate no. 111, Department of Health, Connecticut.

5b. Church records, Sorel; B15 M. Exilda Bergeron. Archives nationales Quebec, Montreal.

5d. Exilda Bergeron Rajotte, death certificate no. 25, Department of Health, Connecticut.

6b. Ubald H.P. Duperry, birth record no. 2934 (1940), City Clerk's office, Fall River, Mass.

6b. Ubald Henri Paul Duperry, baptism certificate, 22 Sept. 1895, Church of the Blessed Sacrament, L.O. Massicotte, Pastor.

6o. Marriage record, State of Maine, Stockholm, Maine, I.Z. Howe, recorder; Edsou K. Labrack, state registrar, (11 Aug. 1959).

6o. Henri H. Duperre, death certificate no. 481, Department of Health, Connecticut.

6m. Marriage record, State of Maine, Stockholm, Maine, I.Z. Howe, recorder; Edsou K. Labrack, state registrar, (11 Aug. 1959).

6d. Henri H. Duperre, death certificate no. 481, Department of Health, Connecticut.

7b. Marriage record, State of Maine, Stockholm, Maine, I.Z. Howe, recorder; Edsou K. Labrack, state registrar, (11 Aug. 1959).

7b. Bertha Levesque, Birth record no. 93-582 (26 Dec. 1942), Clerk's Office, New Sweden, Maine.

7o. Marriage record, State of Maine, Stockholm, Maine, I.Z. Howe, recorder; Edsou K. Labrack, state registrar, (11 Aug. 1959).

7d. Bertha Levesque Duperre, death certificate no. 131, Department of Health, Connecticut.

8b. Felix Rajotte, death certificate no. 111, Department of Health, Connecticut.

8m. Church records, Sorel; M 30 L Rajotte et M. Bergeron. Archives nationales Quebec, Montreal.

9b. Felix Rajotte, death certificate no. 111, Department of Health, Connecticut.

10b. Exilda Bergeron Rajotte, death certificate no. 25, Department of Health, Connecticut.

10m. Church records, Sorel; M 34 Felise Bergeron et Sophie
     Rajotte. Archives nationales Quebec, Montreal.
11b. Exilda Bergeron Rajotte, death certificate no. 25,
     Department of Health, Connecticut.
12o. Ubald H.P. Duperry, birth record no. 2934 (1940), City
     Clerk's office, Fall River, Mass.
12b. Ubald H.P. Duperry, birth record no. 2934 (1940), City
     Clerk's office, Fall River, Mass.
12m. Mary Dupree entry, returned to the clerk of Waterville,
     Maine.
13b. Ubald H.P. Duperry, birth record no. 2934 (1940), City
     Clerk's office, Fall River, Mass.
13b. Marriage record (Henri Duperre, Bertha Levesque), State of
     Maine, Stockholm, Maine, I.Z. Howe, recorder; Edsou K.
     Labrack, state registrar, (11 Aug. 1959).
13d. Mary Dupree entry, returned to the clerk of Waterville,
     Maine.
14. Bertha Levesque, Birth record no. 93-582 (26 Dec. 1942),
    Clerk's Office, New Sweden, Maine.
14b. Marriage certificate, H.R. Hall, deputy, January 1900;
     certified abstract Department of Human Services, Maine (8
     Dec. 2004).
14o. Marriage record (Henri Duperre, Bertha Levesque), State of
     Maine, Stockholm, Maine, I.Z. Howe, recorder; Edsou K.
     Labrack, state registrar, (11 Aug. 1959).
14m. Marriage certificate, H.R. Hall, deputy, January 1900;
     certified abstract Department of Human Services, Maine (8
     Dec. 2004).
14d. Peter Levesque death record no. 120, Clerk's Office,
     Stockholm, Maine.
15. Bertha Levesque, Birth record no. 93-582 (26 Dec. 1942),
    Clerk's Office, New Sweden, Maine.
15b. Marriage record (Henri Duperre, Bertha Levesque), State of
     Maine, Stockholm, Maine, I.Z. Howe, recorder; Edsou K.
     Labrack, state registrar, (11 Aug. 1959).
16m. Church records, Sorel; Archives nationales Quebec,
     Montreal.
17m. ditto

18o. Church records, Sorel; M 30 L Rajotte et M. Bergeron. Archives nationales Quebec, Montreal.

19. Church records, Sorel; M 30 L Rajotte et M. Bergeron. Archives nationales Quebec, Montreal.

20o. Church records, Sorel; M 34 Felise Bergeron et Sophie Rajotte. Archives nationales Quebec, Montreal.a

21. Church records, Sorel; M 34 Felise Bergeron et Sophie Rajotte. Archives nationales Quebec, Montreal.

22o. Church records, Sorel; M 34 Felise Bergeron et Sophie Rajotte. Archives nationales Quebec, Montreal.

23. Church records, Sorel; M 34 Felise Bergeron et Sophie Rajotte. Archives nationales Quebec, Montreal.

24m. Henri Langlois, compiler, Dictionnaire Genealogique du Madawaska, Repertoires des mariages des paroisses de la valee superieure de la riviere Saint Jean au Nouveau Brunswick (Saint Basile, Madawaska, Canada: Ernest Lang, 1971).

25m. ditto

26. Mary Dupree entry, returned to the clerk of Waterville, Maine.

27. ditto

28b. Peter Levesque death record no. 120, Clerk's Office, Stockholm, Maine.

29b. Peter Levesque death record no. 120, Clerk's Office, Stockholm, Maine.

30. Town record, Clerk's Office, Caribou, Maine.

31. ditto

32m. Church records, Sorel; Le Programme de recherche en demographie historique (PRDH), No. 355683.

33m. ditto

48m. Church records, Riviere du Loup; Archives nationales Quebec, Montreal.

49m. ditto

64m. Church records, Sorel; Le Programme de recherche en demographie historique (PRDH), No. 321936.
65m. ditto

98o. Church records, St. Charles de Bellechasse; Archives nationales Quebec, Montreal.
98m. Church records, St. Charles de Bellechase; Archives nationales Quebec, Montreal.
99m. ditto

196m. Church records, Montmagny, PRDH No. 223280; Archives nationales Quebec, Montreal.
197m. ditto

128o. Church records, Quebec, PRDH No. 67929; Archives nationales Quebec, Montreal.
128m. ditto
129m. ditto

256m. Church records, Quebec, PRDH No. 67075; Archives nationales Quebec, Montreal.
257m. ditto

392m. Church records, Montmagny, PRDH No. 136480; Archives nationales Quebec, Montreal.
393m. ditto

514m. Church records, Quebec, PRDH No. 66340; Archives nationales Quebec, Montreal.
515m. ditto

784m. Church records, Montmagny, PRDH No. 26237; Archives nationales Quebec, Montreal.
785m. ditto

1568m. Contrat de mariage, No. 2777, Archives notariales; PRDH No. 94701; Archives nationales Quebec, Montreal.
1569m. ditto

3136m. Church records, Quebec, PRDH No. 66405; Archives
nationales Quebec, Montreal.
3137m. ditto

6274m. Church records, Quebec, PRDH No. 66320; Archives
nationales Quebec, Montreal.
6275m. ditto

12,548 through 12,551: Sources: "Dictionnaire genealogique
des familles canadiennes depuis la fondation de la
colonie jusqu'a nos jours" by Cyprien Tanguay,
"Dictionnaire genealogique des familles du Quebec: des
origines a 1730" by Rene Jette.

PEDIGREE CHARTS

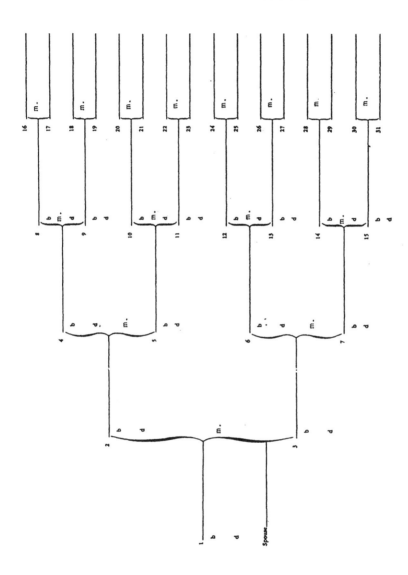

Rajotte-Duperre Genealogy

Pedigree Chart

(See Appendix V for source citations.)

1 Denise M. Rajotte
b
d

2 Bruno J. Rajotte
b 3 July 1914
  St. Germain, Canada
d 3 Oct. 2001
  Bristol, Conn.5

m. 26 April 1947
Bristol, Conn.

3 Lucille A. Duperre
b
d

4 Felix Rajotte
b 14 Dec. 1871
  St. Germain
d 10 April 1952
  Bristol, Conn.

m. 8 Jan. 1895

5 Exilda Bergeron
b 13 Jan. 1875
  Sorel, Canada
d 22 Jan. 1952
  Bristol, Conn.

6 Ubald H.P. Duperry
b 22 Sept. 1895
  Fall River, Mass.13
d 13 Nov. 1974
  Bristol, Conn.

m. 23 June 1919
N.Caribou, Me.14

7 Bertha Levesque
b 1 Nov. 1900
  New Sweden, Me.
d 28 March 196715
  Bristol, Conn.

8 Louis Rajotte
b Canada
m. 16 Aug. 1859
d Canada

9 Marie Bergeron
b Canada
d

10 Felix Bergeron
b Sorel, Canada
m. 8 April 1872
d Sorel, Canada 23

11 Sophie Rajotte
b Sorel, Canada
d

12 Michel Duperry
b Canada
d

13 Marie Levesque
b Canada/Maine
d 1 July 1933
  Fairfield, Me.

14 Thomas Levesque
aka Peter Bishop 29
m. 22 Jan. 1900
d 18 July 1947
  Jane Dasto/Dastou

15 Bertha Levesque

16 Louis Rajotte
m. 14 Nov. 1826

17 Julie Lavallee

18 Ignace Bergeron

19 Christine Ethier

20 Ignace Bergeron

21 Christine Ethier

22 Joseph Rajotte

23 Reine Paul-Hus

24 Michel Duperre

25 Modeste Oulette

26 Jean-B. Levesque

27 Basilise Lavoie

28 Maglore Levesque

29 Archange Landras

30 Guillaume Dastou

31 Apolline Oulet

Spouse

FINAL NOTES

When finally a family's history and genealogy is considered as complete as can be, a copy could be donated to a local or state library or historical society so that if the original is lost, a cataloged, traceable copy still exists. The Library of Congress accepts both homemade and professionally printed genealogies. For more information about submitting a copy to the Library of Congress, contact the Local History & Genealogy Collection Department, Library of Congress, 101 Independence Ave. SE, Washington, D.C. 20540-0660.

No publication is without error. Readers who would like to propose a correction for future editions of *Companions of Champlain* must include a specific citation in (or photocopy thereof) a reliable, verifiable source of the information for the change to be considered. Examples of these are Jette's or Tanguay's works, church repertoires, and civil records. Unsubstantiated genealogies will not suffice.

Please note: If anyone quotes in written form more than a three-word phrase from this work, please use the following as the source reference:

Larson, Denise R. *Companions of Champlain*. Baltimore, Maryland: Clearfield Company, 2008.

Your readers and relatives will thank you—and so will I.

INDEX

CLARIFICATIONS AND ERRATA

The scope of *Companions of Champlain* is an introductory history of New France, genealogical aids to doing research about early French Canadians, and the genealogy of Champlain's Quebecois families through three generations, from the arrival of the first family in 1617 to Samuel de Champlain's death on December 25, 1635. *Companions* was produced in celebration of the 400th anniversary of the founding of Quebec in 1608—the very beginning of French Canadian culture—and as a springboard for readers to begin their personal exploration of family ties to French Canadian history and genealogy.

Many other families of French origin or heritage were established in Quebec after the death of Champlain, and they richly contributed to the French Canadian community (numbering nearly seventy thousand persons in 1760), but it is beyond the limits of this slim volume to include them.

To all the readers who have offered comments, suggestions, and, yes, criticisms, I express my thanks. It is through their eyes that I have seen opportunities for improvement of the text and found clues for more completeness—a vague goal towards which genealogists determinedly strive. This addendum includes a third generation for two members of the Gaspard Boucher family as well as the Marin Boucher family through three generations.

Serendipitously, this 2016 revision of *Companions* comes during the year of the 350th anniversary of the first official census taken in Canada, completed in 1666. The 400th anniversary of the arrival of the first permanent French settlers in New France, the Louis Hebert family, comes in 2017. This truly is a good time to remember our French Canadian roots.

* * *

The name Canada is believed to have been derived by the French from the Huron-Iroquois word *kanata*, which denotes a village or community. Jacques Cartier used the term in 1534 when referring to Stadacona, an Indian settlement near the site of present-day Quebec City. "Canada" appears on the 1638 Robert's

Merchants' Map of the St. Lawrence River area, setting it apart from l'Acadie to the east.

The name Quebec, which the French also rendered as Kébec and Quebecq, is from the Algonquin word for the place where a river narrows. "Quebecq" appeared on a 1601 map by Guillaume Levasseur.

The name Acadia is the English version of Acadie, the French name for the part of New France that is now known as Nova Scotia, New Brunswick, and parts of the Maritimes. "Larcadie" appeared on a 1548 map by Gastaldi. The area is said to have been named by explorer Giovanni da Verrazano, who was reminded of the beauty of Arcadia (note the "r") in Greece when he saw the shores of the New World. Another theory is that the name was based on the Native American word *akadie*, which indicates a place with an abundance of a resource.

Entries in the family genealogies that state that a person died before 1666 refer to the census that was completed in that year. Intendant Talon personally participated in enumerating the French inhabitants of Canada. The census was the first one taken in New France. It revealed that there were more than five hundred families living in and around Quebec, Montreal, and Trois Rivieres. The total French population was tallied at 3,215.

* * *

Addition to References: Leboeuf, J. Arthur. *Complement au Dictionnaire genealogique Tanguay*. Montreal: Societe genealogique canadienne francaise, 1963.

* * *

Errata:
Page 14: Second to last line, omit second *and*
Page 15: Second paragraph, omit *with*, i.e., portrayed using
Page 27: Third paragraph, substitute *women* for *ladies*; fourth paragraph: substitute *throw* for first use of *through*
Page 91: Change II-i to II-ii. (Louis Delaunay)
Page 97: in III-ii., replace second *Guyon* with *married*
Page 142: in II-x., change 1677 to 1672
Page 148: in III-x., change Louis to Louise
Page 153: in III-ix., complete date to read 1717.

Generation III is hereby added to II-iii. Pierre Boucher, son of Gaspard Boucher and Nicole (Page 80):

II-iii.   Pierre Boucher married 1648 Marie-Madeleine Chretienne.

The child of Pierre and Madeleine (Generation III):

III-i.   Jacques Boucher, baptized 11 Dec. 1649 Trois Rivieres, died as a youth.

Pierre married 1652 Jeanne Crevier.

The children of Pierre and Jeanne (Generation III):

III-i.   Pierre Boucher, born 18 Aug. 1653 Trois Rivieres, married 1683 Charlotte Denis.

III-ii.   Marie Ursule Boucher, baptized 8 March 1655 Trois Rivieres, married 1667 Rene Gauthier.

III-iii.   Lambert Boucher, born and baptized 12 August 1656 Trois Rivieres, married 1693 Marguerite Vauvril.

III-iv.   Ignace Boucher, born 17 January 1659 Trois Rivieres, married 1694 Marie-Anne Margane.

III-v.   Madeleine Boucher, born ca. 1661, married 1680 Pierre-Noel LeGardeur.

III-vi.   Marguerite Boucher, born 26 July 1663 Trois Rivieres, married 1687 Nicolas Daneau.

III-vii.   Phillippe Boucher, born 19 Dec. 1665 Trois Rivieres, became a priest.

III-viii.   Jean Boucher, born 6 Feb. 1667 Trois Rivieres, married 1692 Francoise-Claire Charet.

III-ix.   Rene Boucher, baptized 18 June 1668 Montreal, married 1705 Francoise Mailhot.

III-x.   Jeanne Boucher, born 5 Dec. 1670, baptized 8 April 1671 Boucherville, married 1695 Jacques Charles de Sabrevois.

III-xi.   Louise Boucher, Jeanne's twin, born and baptized same date and place as Jeanne. No marriage found.

III-xii.   Nicolas Boucher, born 14 Nov. 1672, became a priest.

III-xiii.   Jean-Baptiste Boucher, born 6 Dec. 1673 Boucherville, married 1710 Therese Hertel.

III-xiv. Jacques Boucher, Jean-Baptiste's twin, born same date, died 1688.

III-xv. Genevieve Boucher, born 19 Aug. 1676 Boucherville, joined a religious order.

Generation III is hereby added to II-viii. Madeleine Boucher, daughter of Gaspard Boucher and Nicole (Page 81):

II-viii. Madeleine Boucher, born ca. 1634, married 1647 Urban Beaudry.

The children of Madeleine and Urban (Generation III):

III-i. Marie Beaudry, baptized 11 Dec. 1650 Trois Rivieres, married 1670 Jacques Lefebvre.

III-ii. Joseph Beaudry, born 13 Nov. 1653 Quebec.

III-iii. Guillaume Beaudry, born 15 Sept. 1655 Quebec, married 1682 Jeanne Soulard.

III-iv. Jeanne Beaudry, born 17 July 1659 Trois Rivieres, married 1672 Jacques Dugay.

III-v. Madeleine Beaudry, born 19 Nov. 1661 Trois Rivieres, married 1681 Jean de Puybaro.

III-vi. Marguerite Beaudry, born 21 March 1665 Trois Rivieres, married 1687 Francois Poisson.

III-vii. Francoise Beaudry, baptized 3 Feb. 1668 Trois Rivieres, married 1691 Jacques Rondeau.

III-viii. Marie-Madeleine Beaudry, born 6 July 1671 Trois Rivieres, married 1698 Jacques Hubert.

III-ix. Joseph Beaudry, born 17 Oct. 1673 Trois Rivieres, married 1706 Marie-Francoise LeClerc.

III-x. Jacques Beaudry, baptized 13 Sept. 1676 Trois Rivieres.

III-xi. Anne Beaudry, baptized 24 June 1680 Trois Rivieres, married 1704 Jean Bougret.

The Marin Boucher Family

I. Marin Boucher, a relative of Gaspard Boucher, possibly a brother, married in France 1611 or 1625 (records differ) Julienne Barry/Baril. Marin was a mason. He arrived in Quebec in 1634. Of the seven children of Marin and Francoise, only one survived:

II. Francois Boucher married 3 Sept 1641 in Quebec Florence Gareman, daughter of Pierre Gareman and Madeleine Charlot.

The children of Francois and Florence (Generation III):

III-i.   Jean Boucher, born 1643, died before 1666.

III-ii.   Bènoit Boucher, born ca. 1645. No marriage recorded.

III-iii. Elisabeth Boucher, baptized 17 March 1646, married1659 Denis Guyon.

III-iv.   Pierre Boucher, baptized 29 Sept. 1648, married 1671/1672 Helene Gaudry.

III-v.   Marin/Marie Boucher, born 1650, died before 1666.

III-vi.   Marie Boucher, born 30 Oct. 1652, married 1672 Antoine Chaudillon.

III-vii. Florence Boucher, born 1654, died before 1666.

III-viii. Charles Boucher, baptized 7 April 1658, married 1685 Marguerite-Agnes Pelletier.

III-ix.   Denis Boucher, baptized 11 April 1660, married 1689 Jeanne Miville.

III-x.   Michel Boucher, baptized May 1661, married 1695 Madeleine Huot.

III-xi.   Francoise Boucher, baptized 6 April 1664, married 1686 Nicolas Thibault.

III-xii. Michel Boucher, baptized 1666, married 19 April 1700 in St. Augustin, Genevieve Amiot.

Marin Boucher married 1629/1632 Perrine Malet/Mallet of Courgeon, Mortagne, Perche, France, daughter of Pierre Malet and Jacqueline Liger.

The children of Marin and Perrine (Generation II):

II-i.   Louis-Marin Boucher, baptized 1630 in France.

II-ii.   Jean-Galeran Boucher, baptized 1633 in France, married
         1661 in Chateau-Richer Marie Leclerc.
         The children of Jean-Galeran and Marie (Generation III):
         III-i.   Marie Boucher, born 26 Feb. 1663 Chateau-
                   Richer, married 1675 Jacques Thiboutot. She
                   married 1688 Francois Autin.
         III-ii.   Pierre Boucher, born 8 Nov. 1664 Chateau-
                   Richer, married 1695 Marie-Anne Michaud.
         III-iii. Philippe Boucher, born 12 Dec. 1666 Chateau-
                   Richer, married 1693 Marie-Anne Mignier.
         III-iv.   Marguerite Boucher, born and died 1669.
         III-v.   Marie-Madeleine Boucher, born 21 June 1670
                   L'Ange-Gardien, married 1688 Jean Lavoie.
         III-vi.   Catherine-Gertrude Boucher, born 24 Feb. 1673
                   Riviere-Ouelle, died 1690 Quebec.
         III-vii. Marie-Anne Boucher, born 28 Feb. 1675
                   Quebec, married 1692 Francois Duval.
         III-viii. Francois Boucher, 3 Feb. 1677 Quebec, married
                   1701 Jeanne Gaudreau.
II-iii. Francoise Boucher, baptized 22 June 1636 Quebec,
         married 1650 Jean Plante.
         The children of Francoise and Jean (Generation III):
         III-i.   Claude Plante, born 26 January 1653 Quebec,
                   married 1678 Marie Patenaude.
         III-ii.   Marie-Francoise Plante, baptized 1855 Quebec,
                   married 1676 Nicolas Paquin.
         III-iii. Jacques Plante, born ca. 1657, married 1686
                   Francoise Turcot. He married 1696 Genevieve
                   Duchene/Duchesneau.
         III-iv.   Georges Plante, born ca. 1659, married 1685
                   Marguerite Crepeau.
         III-v.   Jean Plante, born ca. 1661, married 1687
                   Mathurine Delugre/Leugre. He married 1699
                   Suzanne Lefebvre.
         III-vi.   Thomas Plante, born 17 January 1664 Chateau-
                   Richer, married 1687 Marie-Marthe Paillereau.
         III-vii. Pierre Plante, born 7 April 1666 Chateau-Richer,
                   married 1691 Marguerite Patenaude.

III-viii. Francois Plante, born 3 Dec. 1668 Chateau-Richer, married 1694 Louise Berard. He married 1700 Marie-Anne Coignac.

III-ix. Genevieve Plante, born 20 April 1671 Chateau-Richer, married 1689 Jacques Cauchon/Cochon.

III-x. Angelique Plante, born 9 January 1673 Chateau-Richer, married 1690 Michel Chabot.

III-xi. Joseph Plante, born 15 Dec. 1674 Chateau-Richer, died 1730. No marriage recorded.

III-xii. Unnamed child born and died 14 Nov. 1676.

III-xiii. Louise Plante, baptized 7 January 1678 Chateau-Richer, married 1702 Pierre Coignac/Cognac.

II-iv. Pierre Boucher, baptized 17 Feb. 1639 Quebec, married 1663 in Chateau-Richer Marie-Anne Saint-Denis.

The children of Pierre and Marie-Anne (Generation III):

III-i. Barbe Boucher, baptized Dec. 1663 Chateau-Richer, married 1682 Rene Maheu. Widowed, Barbe married 1686 Georges Cadoret. She married 1711/1712 Louis Jourdain.

III-ii. Pierre Boucher, born and died 1666 Chateau-Richer.

III-iii. Jacques Boucher, born and died 1667.

III-iv. Marie Boucher, born 11 Aug. 1668 Ste-Famille Ile d'Orleans, married 1689 Jean Mignault/Mignot.

III-v. Jean Boucher, born 14 Jan. 1671 Ste-Famille Ile d'Orleans, married 1696 Angelique Guay.

III-vi. Pierre Boucher, born 4 May 1673 Ste-Famille Ile d'Orleans, married 1697 Marie-Madeleine Dancosse.

III-vii. Angelique Boucher, born 27 Oct. 1676 Ste-Famille Ile d'Orleans, married 1697 Louis Dube.

III-viii. Charles Boucher, born 1679, married 1704 Marie-Anne Ouellet.

III-ix. Marie-Therese Boucher, born 9 Jan 1683 Chateau-Richer, married 1704 Pierre Dube.

III-x. Genevieve Boucher, born 12 Sept. 1685 Chateau-Richer, married 1706 Laurent Dube.

III-xi.   Prisque Boucher, born 22 April 1689 Chateau-Richer, married 1712 Francoise Miville.

III-xii. Marguerite Boucher, born 12 May 1692 Chateau-Richer, had a child, Marguerite, 11 March 1724 in Lauzon; father unknown.

II-v.   Madeleine Boucher, baptized 4 Aug. 1641 Quebec, married 1655 in Quebec, Louis Houde.

The children of Madeleine and Louis (Generation III):

III-i.   Jean Houde, born ca. 1658, married 1678 Anne Rouleau.

III-ii. Francoise Houde, born ca. 1660, died 1665.

III-iii. Louis Houde, born 28 Sept. 1662 Chateau-Richer, married 1685 Marie Lemay.

III-iv. Gervais Houde, born 23 Dec. 1664 Chateau-Richer, married 1689 Catherine DeNevers.

III-v.   Jacques Houde, born 24 March 1667 Ste-Famille Ile d'Orleans, married 1681/1692 Marie-Louise Beaudet.

III-vi. Marie Houde, born 6 Aug. 1669 Ste-Famille Ile d'Orleans, married 1685 Issac-Joseph Garnier.

III-vii. Claude Houde, born 11 July 1671 Ste-Famille Ile d'Orleans, married 1695 Marie-Madeleine Lemay.

III-viii. Louise Houde, born ca. 1673, married 1681 Charles Lemay.

III-ix. Marie-Anne Houde, born 22 Dec. 1674 Ste-Famille Ile d'Orleans, died 1675.

III-x.   Louis Houde, born 23 Dec. 1675 Ste-Famille Ile d'Orleans, married 1697 Anne-Ursule Bisson/Buisson.

III-xi. Joseph Houde, born 25 June 1678 Ste-Famille Ile d'Orleans, married 1697 Louise-Angelique Garnier.

III-xii. Simon Houde, born 30 May 1680 Ste-Famille Ile d'Orleans, married 1703 Marie Frechet/Frichet.

III-xiii. Etienne Houde, born 4 April 1682 Ste-Famille Ile d'Orleans, married 1708 Elisabeth-Ursule DeNevers.

III-xiv. Marie-Angelique Houde, birth date unknown, married 1705 Guillaume Rognon.

II-vi. Marie Boucher, born 11 April 1644, married 1656 in Quebec, Charles Gaudin/Godin.

The children of Marie and Charles (Generation III):

III-i.   Francois G—, born ca. 1659, died 1662.

III-ii.   Marie G—, born 27 April 1662 Chateau-Richer, married 1682 Louis Goulet. She married 1687 Pierre Denis.

III-iii. Genevieve G—, born 1 Oct. 1663 Chateau-Richer, married 1689 Francois Gariepy.

III-iv.   Marguerite G—, born 8 March 1665 Chateau-Richer, married 1687 Guillaume Tardif.

III-v.   Ursule G—, born 9 June 1667 Chateau-Richer, married 1689 Denis Quentin.

III-vi.   Charles G—, born 15 Nov. 1668 Chateau-Richer, married 1689 Marie-Madeleine Perron.

III-vii. Anne G—, born 25 Dec. 1670 L'Ange-Gardien, married 1698 Jean Perron.

III-viii. Catherine G—, born 23 April 1672 L'Ange-Gardien, married 1694 Pierre Dumesnil.

III-ix.   Madeleine G—, born 11 Oct. 1673 L'Ange-Gardien, married 1698 Jacques Desnoux.

III-x.   Pierre G—, born 30 June 1675 L'Ange-Gardien, married 1704 Anne Matheu.

III-xi.   Angelique G—, baptized 24 June 1677 L'Ange-Gardien, married 1695/1698 Jacques Amelot.

III-xii. Jean-Francois G—, born 30 Jan. 1679 L'Ange-Gardien, married 1705 Genevieve Lefrancois.

III-xiii. Alexis G—, born 4 April 1680 L'Ange-Gardien, married 1706 Madeleine Jacob.

III-xiv. Louise G—, born 31 Jan. 1682 L'Ange-Gardien, married 1705 Charles Vesinat/Vezina.

III-xv.   Charlotte G—, born 18 Sept. 1683 L'Ange-Gardien, married 1717 Vincent Guillot.

III-xvi. Francoise G—, born 10 April 1685 L'Ange-Gardien, married 1704 Martin Page.

III-xvii. Antoine G—, born 2 Sept. 1688 L'Ange-Gardien, married 1712 Catherine Jacob.

II-vii.   Guillaume Boucher, baptized 5 May 1647 in Quebec,
          married 1672 Marguerite-Jeanne Thibault/Thibaut.
          The child of Guillaume and Marguerite (Generation III):
          III-i.   Marguerite Boucher, baptized 27 Oct. 1675
                   Chateau-Richer, married 1692 Francois Laberge.